Different Sexual Worlds

Different Sexual Worlds

Contemporary Case Studies of Sexuality

DICK SKEEN

LEXINGTON BOOKS
Lanham • Boulder • New York • Oxford

LEXINGTON BOOKS

Published in the United States of America
by Lexington Books
4720 Boston Way, Lanham, Maryland 20706

12 Hid's Copse Road
Cumnor Hill, Oxford OX2 9JJ, England

British Library Cataloguing in Publication Information Available

The 1991 edition of this book was previously catalogued by
the Library of Congress as follows:

Skeen, Dick.
    Different sexual worlds : contemporary case studies of sexuality / by Dick Skeen.
        p.   cm.
    1. Sex customs—United States—Case studies. 2. Homosexuality—United States—
Case studies. 3. Sexual deviation—United States—Case studies. 4. Sex instruction
for youth—United States—Problems, exercises, etc. I. Title.
HQ18.U5S56   1991
306.7'0973—dc20   90–49596
                                                                                      CIP

ISBN 0-7391-0030-0 (pbk. : alk. paper)
ISBN: 978-0-7391-0030-1
Printed in the United States of America

In memory of Carrie Rayma Skeen

October 18, 1984–August 1, 1992

Her light will always shine in my heart.

Contents

Acknowledgments xi

Preface for Educators xiii

Introduction for Students xv

A Beginning Note xix

1. **Beyond Dependency**
   Case Study of Libby Williams 1

   The story of a woman who entered a traditional marriage that
   ended traumatically and who then had to explore different sexual
   options in order to find personal satisfaction.
   Topics: emotional dependency, early marriage, gang rape, suicide of
   a spouse, sexual experimentation, quality of relationships, and
   sexual awareness.

2. **Trying to Leave a Traditional Life-style**
   Case Study of Stan Fitzgerald 15

   This man chose to leave his family's traditional Catholic life-style.
   The case study analyzes the problems he had in pursuing a new
   life-style.
   Topics: adolescent sexuality, peer groups, virginity, romantic
   fantasies versus actual relationships, value clarification, sexual
   self-esteem, and impotence.

3. **Sexual Experimentation Leading Finally to a More**
   Traditional Relationship
   Case Study of Nick Orren 31

   This man experimented with a wide variety of sexual life-styles and
   ultimately returned to a fairly traditional marriage.
   Topics: self-confidence, sexual confidence, sexual experimentation,

drugs and sex, group sex, abortion, life-structures, contrasting
relationships, sexuality as a developmental process, and sexual
maturity.

4. **Growing up as a Lesbian**
   Case Study of Tori Montgomery 49

The story of a woman who discovered she was gay and a discussion
of how being a lesbian has influenced and shaped her life.
Topics: emerging lesbian feelings, social stigma, the power of labels,
loneliness, coming out, emotional and sexual satisfaction,
managing a socially unapproved sexual identity, the social
construction of sexuality, lesbian versus heterosexual perspectives,
and gay issues.

5. **Living a Life of Committed Celibacy within a Sexual Society**
   Case Study of Father Patrick Graddy 63

This man chose to become a Catholic priest. He discusses how he
has dealt with the issues of celibacy and sexuality within our
sexual society.
Topics: self-image, adolescent uncertainty, religion and celibacy,
intellectual versus emotional growth, the power of choice,
choosing sexual meanings, historical celibacy, and utilizing sexual
insights.

6. **A Journey into the World of Prostitution and Beyond**
   Case Study of Jennifer Bryce 79

The story of a woman from an upper-middle-class family who,
during her youth, escaped from her family and became a
prostitute. The case study analyzes her experiences as a prostitute
and how she adjusted to leaving that profession.
Topics: the abuse of children, prostitution, sexual extremes,
impersonal sex, strippers, social stigmas, battered women,
therapy, and rebuilding a sexual identity.

7. **Radical Midlife Changes**
   Case Study of Kevin Krammer 99

A study of a professor who led a traditional life until age forty-five
and who then decided his life was not much of a success. He
entered the realm of financial investment and became wildly
successful. He believes success radically changed his sense of self
and his sexuality.
Topics: fear of mediocrity, midlife crisis, open relationships, risk
taking, power-sexuality, success and sexual identity, and aging
and sexuality.

8. **A Life of Contrasting Options**
   Case Study of Ed Fogelberg 117

   This is the story of a gay man who has AIDS. An analysis is
      offered of his sexual development and how he is living with this
      deadly disease.
   Topics: male homosexuality, causes of sexual orientation, sexual
      experimentation, AIDS, the grief process, the gay subculture,
      and appreciation of life.

9. **Sex, Drugs, and Rock and Roll**
   Case Study of Terry Grant 139

   This man led a successful rock and roll band, but his deep
      involvement with sex and drugs has proved problematic.
   Topics: sexual alienation, career shaping sexuality, scoring
      sexually, emotional detachment, drug abuse, image construction,
      and authentic experience.

10. **Living with Incest**
    Case Study of Joanne Sheridan 157

    A story of an incest survivor who has undergone extensive therapy
       and is learning how to develop a satisfying sexual relationship.
    Topics: family dynamics, sexual abuse of children, guilt, sexual
       disclosure, betrayal, raging anger, sexual therapy, and support
       networks.

Epilogue 177

About the Author 181

Acknowledgments

The professional life of an academic sociologist can be a rich and varied journey. My life has been blessed with many special people. First I want to thank my students at Northern Arizona University who challenge and inspire me.

Professor Ray Cuzzort at the University of Colorado must be thanked for sharing his passion for humanity, social structures, and life itself. John Murphy at the Flinn Foundation must be acknowledged for encouraging many of us to dream the big dream. Chancellor Joseph Cox of the Oregon University system deserves recognition as a visionary administrator.

Special thanks for editorial and conceptual support go to: Joe Shaffer, Dan Darpino, Rick Kroc, Evelyn Wong, Robbie Bergman, Terry Wing, Joe Boles, and Ilana Landes. Sage counsel was also received from professorial colleagues: Florence Karlstrom, Rich Fernandez, Phyllis Schiller, Mike Brown, Kooros Mahmoudi, Bryan Short, Doug Degher, Warren Lucas, and Margaret Zahn. My graduate research assistants Ken Brewer and Mark Templeton proved invaluable. I also appreciate the encouragement Northern Arizona University provides for research and publication and the university's dedicated office staff, Debbie, Kathy, and Lucie.

All of the staff at Lexington Books have been more than helpful, particularly senior editor Margaret Zusky and production editor Lyri Merrill. Special thanks to Serena Leigh for bringing this second edition to life.

My wife, Janet, has been quite supportive and I have received much encouragement from the P's and Rayma.

Many thanks to James Fry and my teaching assistants for their comments, insights, and overall enthusiasm for this project. Melanie has been a peach.

Finally, I would like to express my gratitude to each of the participating subjects for sharing their intimate lives so graciously. The strengths in this book sprang from them; the shortcomings are alas mine.

Preface for Educators

There are so many books already available for courses on human sexuality; why would anyone want to write another? Of course there is always pressure to publish or a fairly understandable desire to make some money, but this book was not written for those purposes. The ten case studies in this text were written to help college students understand how the academically separated areas of human sexuality integrate in real individual lives.

These case studies extend the kind of sex education provided by the standard college texts on human sexuality. Most sexuality texts provide students with chapters analyzing particular dimensions of human sexual activity. By reading these case studies, students can gain an integrated perspective on human sexuality as well as on their own sexual development.

I believe this book represents a dramatic new departure from current college texts on sexuality because while it deals with the issues covered in a standard text, it also shows precisely how these issues are actually integral in the lives of real people. At the end of each case study, an analysis section links key developmental issues with contemporary literature on that issue. These analysis sections allow students with particular interests or issues of their own to pursue them further. Following each analysis section there are discussion questions designed to encourage students individually and collectively to explore an extended range of developmental issues pertaining to human sexuality. If your students take the time to consider these discussion questions, their understanding of sexual development will increase dramatically. This new approach makes the book a perfect companion to most of the standard texts available.

For the thousands of students who have taken my human sexuality courses at the University of Colorado, the University of Oklahoma, and Northern Arizona University, these case studies have provided profound and important insights into the development of sexual relationships. My students tell me that the cases have been interesting to read, and have dramatically increased their understanding of how we as humans come to construct the web of social meanings that compose our sexuality.

In teaching sexuality classes ranging from twenty students to twelve hundred students, I have found these case studies useful in different ways. In smaller classes they can be incorporated directly into ongoing class discussions as a valuable learning tool. With larger classes, discussions are often limited by the sheer size of the group; in this context, I have found the case studies extremely useful for outside-of-class discussion groups of eight to ten students or recitation sections.

Several of my colleagues teaching human sexuality courses at other institutions were initially skeptical about how these case studies would fit in with their varied course formats and texts. After trying a case study or two, most found that they added a lively and provocative stimulus to their courses. For professors who enjoy exploring new and innovative ways to integrate concepts and ideas, these case studies will prove interesting.

For me, teaching is a continuous process of refinement and innovation. I look forward to hearing from you to learn how *Different Sexual Worlds* affected your course on human sexuality.

Introduction for Students

What does sex mean to you? Who or what helps you define your sexuality? Have you ever wondered what a prostitute thinks about sex? Have you ever wondered how a celibate priest deals with his sexual feelings? In your opinion what would constitute a great sexual relationship?

If these questions seem either important or intriguing, you will find this book extremely useful in extending your understanding of the social processes that shape everyone's sexuality.

I was in one of those trendy comedy clubs recently, and a young comedian was developing a joke about a male and female horse that had just finished having sex together. As the joke progressed, the male horse was trying to figure out what his recent sexual encounter "meant." Was it true love, or did she have eyes for other horses? Did she think he, as a horse, was adequate? Was she just using him for a quick romp in the hay? And so on. The audience found this fairly funny simply because nobody believes that horses get this complicated in thinking about their sex lives. But of course we humans do. And the variety of meanings and complexity found in human sexuality will amaze you. Our sexuality is an important dimension of our humanity. Sexuality is often intertwined with some of our most significant and positive feelings of loving, caring, pleasure, and commitment. Conversely, one's sexuality can also generate the most extreme feelings of rejection, unworthiness, inadequacy, and personal alienation.

This book contains ten case studies that show how these contributing individuals experienced and developed their sexual lives. The focus throughout this book is on *understanding what sex means* in people's lives, and on understanding the diversity of sexual life-styles that are possible.

The subjects included in this book represent a wide variety and were chosen from more than two hundred subjects I interviewed about their sexuality: the spectrum of human sexual development is far greater and more complex than most of us initially suspect. This diversity is presented in actual lives so that you can see what a priest and a prostitute might have in common or how a rock and roll star might sacrifice personalized sex for flash. The point is that by studying many different sexual life-styles, we begin to understand the way sexual meanings are constructed in our own lives.

The only biases that have intruded in these case studies are my own against coercive or violent sex and the caveat that I believe sex should occur between mutually consenting adults. The book includes a case of an older and very successful businessman, a young woman who discovered early in adolescence that she was a lesbian, a gay man who is currently dying of AIDS, a celibate Catholic priest, a professor who led a very rambunctious and radical sexual life, and a woman who entered a traditional marriage and later found it highly unsatisfactory. Included are the old and the relatively young, the sexually fulfilled as well as the sexually frustrated. This selection of subjects provides a broad sampling of sexual life-styles found in contemporary America.

Each of the ten case studies included in this book is organized in the following fashion. First, the subject's life is reviewed chronologically, beginning with his or her earliest recollected experiences and progressing to the present time. Each subject has described his or her sexual experiences, thoughts, and feelings about those experiences. Every attempt has been made to preserve the subject's viewpoint, using the subject's own words and following the subject's own chronology except where necessary changes were made to ensure the subject's anonymity. All of the subjects reviewed their case histories and were allowed to make changes to preserve their anonymity. In this sense, the quotes are more refined than those usually found in casual conversation.

Following each subject's case, there is an analysis section in which I have identified significant issues from each case and integrated those issues with selections from the current literature. In this way we can see how each individual case study is linked to a much larger body of available sexuality literature. Following each brief analysis section is a short bibliography that will allow those of you who are interested to pursue any of the topics mentioned in the analysis section with more vigor and thoroughness.

Following the analysis sections are topical discussion questions that probe issues raised in each case studied. Many of these issues have direct bearing on the lives of college students. My students have found these discussion questions to be the most valuable part of this entire project. They enjoyed exploring the issues raised in this section and frequently found themselves in highly animated debate. I believe that anyone who seriously considers these discussion questions, particularly as they affect his or her own life, will gain a significant new understanding of human sexuality.

Now that these case studies are available in book form, it is my sincere hope that they will prove as interesting to you as they have to my students.

A Beginning Note

When faced with sex we readily abandon respect for diversity and choice, we neglect any duty to understand human motivation and potentialities, and fall back on received pieties and authoritarian methods. The result can be devastating for those who are forced to live on the margins of social acceptability—and inhibitive for those who do not.

—Jeffrey Weeks, *Sexuality and its Discontents*. (London: Routledge & Kegan Paul Ltd., 1985), 53.

While the term "erotocentrism" is now being used in contemporary discussions of sexuality, it is not yet listed in dictionaries. My students asked, so here is my definition:

Erotocentrism—an overriding belief that one's sexual behavior and attitude is superior to all others and that one's own sexuality is the standard by which all others should be judged.

1
Beyond Dependency: Case Study of Libby Williams

Libby Williams, a wholesome, poised woman in her late forties, still retains the youthful charm and disarming smile that she had as a high school cheerleader. However, the last twenty-five years of her life have seasoned this once naive young woman and helped her emerge as the self-assured yet sensitive dean of a large state college.

Libby grew up in Tillamook, a small, rural town in northwestern Oregon where her father worked steadily as a heavy equipment operator while her mother stayed home. Libby spent most of her childhood raising her retarded younger brother, George. For many years she lovingly cared for him. With her father working long hours and frequently out "with the boys," her mother kept to herself, sometimes not even speaking to the family for days at a time.

Until Libby was seven, her paternal grandmother lived with the family. Libby remembers many early experiences when her grandmother showered her with warmth and affection. Her grandmother first noticed Libby's intelligence. Even today, Libby believes she became an academic because of her grandmother's support for her school work. Her grandmother finally moved out because she could no longer stand the moody, silent periods and the strict and all-consuming moral self-righteousness of Libby's mother.

> My mother was an ultraconservative Baptist. She always feared the wrath of God. Her unending concern was to live a morally upright life. She saw evil lurking everywhere, in everything. She was a most unhappy person. As children, my brother and I were subject to the strictest code of conduct. I know this sounds hard to understand today, particularly in this environment [gestures at the campus outside her office window], but back then I was never allowed to see a movie or drink soda pop or wear jewelry, pants, or makeup. My father basically ignored my mother, which I think made her all the more strict with us. She was an extremely harsh disciplinarian with a bad temper. She even slapped George around if she felt he had sinned. I think, in some unconscious way, she felt George's retardation was her own punishment for sinning.

Her grandmother's departure crushed Libby. The daily routine of taking care of her brother became more consuming. School was her only chance to explore new worlds beyond her restrictive home life. She excelled academically, and eventually her teachers suggested that she transfer to a larger junior high school in a town nearby. Her mother rejected this suggestion. Libby recalled feeling no anger, just "disappointed." Shortly after this happened, Libby's parents separated. Libby wanted to leave with her father and he was amenable to taking her; however, her mother insisted that if her father took her, he must also take George. Since her father was unwilling to take George, he left without Libby. Again, Libby reported not feeling angry, only "disappointed."

During seventh and eighth grade, Libby continued to care for her brother while avoiding her mother's wrath whenever possible. She continued to do exceptionally well in school and, being attractive, was often asked out. Knowing her mother would never allow her to date, she always politely declined.

Libby's sexual education at home was nearly nonexistent. The only ideas communicated at home about sexuality were negative ones, based on her mother's conservative religious feelings. She learned about menstruation from her girlfriends, and she never witnessed any affection at home between her parents. The only explicit sexual message Libby received at home was when her mother caught her retarded brother, George, touching his genitals. She slapped him around the house repeatedly, telling him what an evil, sinful little boy he was.

As a child Libby never masturbated. She came to believe that sex was primarily of interest to men and that women participated to please them. In this way, women could use sex to obtain the affections of a man.

In high school, new and exciting things happened. Because Libby had to go to a larger town about thirty miles away for high school, she was able to develop a new social life quite hidden from her mother. She was popular at school. During her senior year, she was elected president of the senior class and became head cheerleader. She also dated the captain of the football team by whom she became pregnant.

> Tommy and I were like the kind of couple that is in every corny movie about high school. He was the big jock type—very good looking. I was the eager, naive cheerleader type. Everyone in school thought we were the perfect couple. Even when I got pregnant, he was still the hero. He told me that we would have to get married right away.

Predictably, Libby's mother became extremely upset. During the ensuing emotional conflict at home, Libby miscarried. However, Tommy kept his promise and married her shortly thereafter. Following graduation, the newlyweds moved to southern Oregon, where Tommy bought a sizable farm. Libby attended a local college where she eventually graduated with honors. Tommy worked hard on the farm and spent a lot of time with his loving wife.

> Marrying Tommy and moving to southern Oregon was like a dream come true. Those first years together were beautiful—wonderful. We were both so much in love. We shared everything. Our first son brought us even closer together. We were such proud parents. You would think we had invented something new.

Although Tommy and Libby lived happily together those first years in Oregon and enjoyed being parents, in hindsight Libby reported that sexually their relationship was not dynamic. Libby had let Tommy have sex to secure his affection. She had also seen Tommy as a means of escape from her mother and the constant care that she had to provide for her brother. Their romantic life together did not include much sexual arousal or satisfaction for Libby; she never had an orgasm with Tommy. Tommy always instigated sex, and her only sexual excitement was giving him pleasure. In the same way that her early life had been consumed with providing support for George, now it was consumed with providing for Tommy, and later their children.

Two years after their first son was born, their relationship started to deteriorate rapidly. They had extended fights during which Tommy would stay in town for a day or two. Tommy made no effort to disguise his emerging involvements with other women. Libby felt helpless and disappointed.

> Tommy started being very depressed. He constantly said he felt trapped. The next four or five years we just rode an emotional roller coaster—up one day and down in the pits the next. He usually was sensitive and caring, but he could be a real bastard sometimes. One night while his brother was staying with us, he asked me to strip so he and his brother could have a look. When I refused, he grabbed me and ripped off my clothes. Then he and his brother had me. [Libby begins crying. She sustained a broken arm during this incident.] He really wanted to degrade me. The saddest part of all was my own insecurity. I put up with this sort of thing without ever getting good and mad at him. I always assumed our problems were my fault.

For the next year, Libby stayed with Tommy and gave birth to another son. Eventually, however, it became too much, and while Tommy was out of town, she left with the kids, writing a note apologizing for the problems she had caused him. Feeling lost, she moved to Eugene and began trying to survive, emotionally and financially. Within a year she had secured a full academic scholarship for graduate work in psychology and began seeing a growth-oriented therapist.

> I underwent some dramatic changes then. I looked in the mirror and said, "You are an untrained older woman with two kids—can you make it alone?" When I knew I could, I felt free and strong.

During this period Libby dated several men. However, she did not become sexually involved with any of them because in some ways she "still felt married." She had not legally or emotionally finished her relationship with Tommy.

Sexually speaking, this period in Libby's life proved to be rather difficult. Libby was interested in meeting new men and getting to know them. Because she was both bright and attractive, several men became quite interested in her as well. However, most of these men did want some sexual contact with her. So far in Libby's life, sex had been only an avenue of pleasing Tommy. At this point, she did not have sexual interests of her own, and she became depressed when most of these men would not continue seeing her without some sort of sexual contact. Since she did not want any sexual contact, her life became a series of short-lived dating situations that usually ended painfully.

Eventually, Tommy asked her to return to the farm. Libby agreed to bring the children down that weekend for a visit; she had high hopes for a major reconciliation, since Tommy had told her how much he missed both her and the children. Arriving one day early, she found him in bed with another woman. When she began to cry, he laughed, saying he had lied about missing her so that she would move back. He had lied in order to give himself a draft deferment (this was the early Vietnam War period).

> I became enraged for the first time in my life. I told him he was a bastard to manipulate me and the kids. I raged. He had never seen me angry before. It hit him hard.

Tommy strode out of the house, roared off in his car, and drove into a telephone pole about a mile away, which killed him instantly.

> I have spent a lot of time thinking about Tommy's suicide. His life was coming unraveled pretty fast. The farm was a financial disaster. He was drinking a lot, he was concerned about the draft, and he probably knew that this was his last chance to get his family back and be in charge of us again. When I blew up at him, it was just the last straw. He had always controlled me, and he could not face losing that control as well as everything else.

Libby returned to Eugene and school where she spent several years trying to put her life back together.

Tommy's suicide hit Libby hard. She had never been very assertive or comfortable expressing her anger. During key decision periods in her life, disappointment seemed to obscure any of her feelings of anger. After Tommy's suicide, she felt that her whole world was shattered; nevertheless, she suspected that her newly emerging feelings of anger signaled the beginning of a new life. Libby gradually realized that her dependency on Tommy had been destructive for her whole family and that ultimately she needed a different kind of relationship.

One of her professors, named Dale, helped her confront her anguish and anger. She and Dale became close friends and eventually lovers.

Dale knew I was attracted to him. Lord knows I needed someone strong and caring to help me pull myself together. He was married, so we were only lovers a couple of times. We actually had more of a friendship than anything else. When I started feeling better about myself I found that we shared a lot academically. He also was great with the kids, which I figured helped them get over their loss too.

Libby liked Dale for many reasons, but she was particularly impressed with his maturity and compassion:

Dale's maturity impressed me. I thought, Here is someone whose own problems will not have to mess me up. He was supportive without being dominant. He was not a father figure, just a close friend who helped immeasurably. I knew I could never marry him, not only because of his wife, but also because he was so much older [sixteen years older]. I began to have a sense of the kind of person that would be good for me.

Sexually, Libby's relationship with Dale was similar to her relationship with Tommy. She cared for Dale, but Dale was far more interested in sex than she was. She had sex with Dale in return for his compassion and help in dealing with Tommy's suicide. Dale helped Libby heal. She recalled that her overall feeling for Dale was similar to the one she used to have for her paternal grandmother, who had been the only adult to show her genuine affection when she was a child.

Shortly after Libby's thirty-second birthday, her relationship with Dale ended amicably. She moved back East to begin work on her Ph.D. with a full academic scholarship to a prestigious university.

During her six years in the Ph.D. program, Libby had several sexual relationships. The most significant relationship involved John, who was also her academic adviser. She took John's graduate seminar her first semester. Often after class, several of the graduate students would go to a local bar for a few drinks. Frequently John would accompany them. A divorcé, John was known to get sexually involved with lots of women, many of them willing graduate students.

After one of these informal bar sessions, Libby found herself alone with John.

The rest of the students left early while he and I were having an extended discussion about behaviorism. Fairly abruptly, both of us started sensing that we had more to discuss than just that. It was like all of a sudden we were looking into each other's eyes. John is an amazing person, but I did not want to become just another one of his women. I let him know I was interested in him without indicating that he should ask me out. We were in that bar a couple of hours, not flirting—more like sparring. He came very close a couple of times to asking me out, but each time I gave him the feeling that I would probably say no. He is no dummy. He picked up all the clues and eventually we separated. The next night I asked him out.

Libby and John became lovers the night of their first date. She described her visit to his apartment by saying,

I sort of felt like I was walking into the lion's den. His apartment was like a typical bachelor pad. He had this black leather furniture all over and this low indirect lighting. It is sort of the decor one sees in *Playboy*. I wanted to be there. I had even left the kids at a friend's for the night, yet the whole feeling to his apartment nearly put me off. I was real nervous and he seemed so relaxed, yet I knew that I wanted to be involved with him.

Libby's relationship with John lasted slightly over two years. They spent much time together, particularly in outdoor sports since both loved to ski and hike. John shared a lot with her, including several discussions about the many women he had known before. She reported that although he became eager to extend their relationship she felt less committed. Rather unexpectedly, John purchased a diamond engagement ring and asked her to marry him. When she declined, their relationship ended. Libby reported feeling "flattered" by John's proposal, but she did not want a long-term relationship with him. She was sorry to see him so deflated. John refused to speak to her after she rejected him.

Libby's relationship with John represented a turning point in her sexual development. Although she still had not had an orgasm, she did feel herself becoming more responsive to him sexually than she had with any other man. She learned how to bring him to orgasm, and since that provided a great deal of pleasure for him, she felt she had more equality in their sexual relationship. Libby also felt that their relationship had been good for her bruised ego. John's reputation for attracting many intelligent, good-looking women and his offer of marriage gave Libby a heightened sense of herself as a desirable and interesting woman.

When she was thirty-eight she obtained her Ph.D. and returned to Oregon. Libby's new faculty position involved extensive research. On one research project, she met Dennis, a graduate research assistant assigned to her project.

Libby described Dennis as "one of the best-looking men I have ever seen. His body ripples with muscles, which is quite a turn on." Dennis had been in the military and, like John, had a reputation for attracting many women. While he was serving in Vietnam, several of his close friends had been killed. In response to his Vietnam experience, he developed an insouciant, live-for-the-present life-style. Although he manifested a playful, nearly carefree attitude, Dennis also acquired a reputation for being one of the brightest and most promising of the research assistants.

While doing research together Dennis and Libby became "buddies." The informal research atmosphere and his playfulness proved to be most conducive to a slowly emerging friendship. Initially, Libby was a sort of confidante to him, and she would often tease him about his involvements with other women. After they had worked together for over two years, Libby became romantically interested in him.

> I think I had always wanted to be more than just buddies, but part of my traditional background said that women should not instigate anything. He was worried that dating might ruin our working relationship. I think we were both surprised at how well it worked out. I made him know that he was number one in my book. I do not think he had ever had as much support and caring as I gave him. He taught me how to laugh again, how to play, how to skip and run naked in the mountains and how life can be ever so rich. He taught me to embrace everything. I remember one day in the woods, how he fell to his knees to smell the pine needles and earth. He was so full of life. His attitude was highly contagious.

Libby and Dennis have now been lovers for over six years. Dennis is helping her enjoy and develop her sexuality.

> I had been [sexually] involved with several men. However, because of my traditional religious upbringing and the older men I

had been with, most of my sex life was a pretty straightforward, wham-bam-thank-you-ma'am type thing. With him [Dennis] it is different. He is confident and assured, but more importantly, he accepts his body and mine. He taught me to love my body. Sex is an important and freeing part of our relationship. He is extremely sensitive, and we have excellent communication between us. He is a responsive lover, and we synchronize easily. I often have multiple orgasms with him, which is exciting for both of us. We just have a good, responsive, and playful sex life. Even the very first time we made love, Dennis noticed that I was not in tune with my own body. He encouraged me to explore my sexuality. It was a fabulous awakening!

Libby feels she has now reached a new phase in her life. Professionally, she has distinguished herself as a professor, a department chair, and now as dean of the college. Her relationship with Dennis is qualitatively different, being both more fulfilling and satisfying than she had ever dreamed possible.

Not long ago Dennis gave me a most sensual massage. First, he slowly undressed me, and then we showered together. Then he carefully heated some scented massage oil and proceeded to slowly stroke and lovingly caress my entire body. He spent almost two hours exploring and sensually rejuvenating my entire physical being. I tingled all over. In every part of my body he made me feel the kind of caring loving person he can be. When we made love afterward, I literally felt myself melting away as a separate person and being joyously consumed in our passionate bonding. These kinds of experiences provide a kind of renewing vitality, and they give me a healthy energy for the other dimensions of my life. Dennis is very special in my life.

However, Libby is not sure what the future holds for herself and Dennis. Dennis's computer business is quite demanding, and her job as dean requires many long hours. Also, Libby feels that she has not finished growing and evolving into the kind of woman that she would like to be. She is not sure how she will grow and change or how those changes might affect her relationship with Dennis. She is fairly certain that she wants to make a long-term commitment with a person like Dennis, if not Dennis, but she is not certain that commitment is in the immediate future. She knows she will never again be the overly dependent and submissive woman she was with Tommy. She also believes that Dennis has significant issues remaining from Vietnam and his early childhood which he wants and needs to address. She remains hopeful that they can both work out these issues while continuing to be supportive, caring, and passionately involved.

ANALYSIS

Emotional Dependency

Since she was raised in a restrictive and intellectually limited family environment, bullied first by her mother and then by Tommy, it seemed improbable that Libby Williams would ultimately develop a dynamic professional career and sexual identity. But she did. In understanding how Libby overcame her emotional dependency, the work of Peele and Brodsky should prove insightful.

In their *Love and Addiction* (1975), they discuss how individuals who are very pliable, overly trusting, unsure of themselves, and lacking in self-confidence are often susceptible to addictive (or what we now term *dependent*) behavior. They go on to say that "love is an ideal vehicle for dependency because it can so exclusively claim a person's consciousness" (Peele 1980, 70). Libby's relationship with Tommy is a classic case of codependency. Libby tolerated a broken arm and gang rape from Tommy while still feeling that she caused most of the problems in their relationship. She even left him a note apologizing when she eventually moved out. When she finally asserted her independence and became angry, his dependency fueled his suicide.

Quality of Relationships

One major issue we will be reviewing in all of these case studies is the quality established in sexual relationships. Although Tommy and Libby's marriage seemed fairly idyllic at first, their codependency proved problematic. Peele provides some interesting criteria for analyzing relationships and distinguishing between those that embrace a positive enactment of love and those that become dependent:

1. Does each lover have a secure belief in his or her own value?
2. Are the lovers improved by their relationship?
3. Do the lovers maintain serious interests outside the relationship, including other meaningful personal relationships?
4. Is the relationship integrated into the totality of the lovers' lives?
5. Are the lovers beyond being possessive or jealous of each other's growth?
6. Are the lovers friends? (Peele and Brodsky 1980, 83–84)

Though dependency is not a black-and-white issue, using these criteria shows that Libby and Tommy's relationship can hardly be viewed as healthy. For students who are interested, the authors' last chapter, "From Addiction [Dependency] to Love," contains several insightful suggestions on how to build a supportive rather than a dependent relationship.

Sexual Awareness

Libby Williams's ability to experience and understand her own sexuality emerged slowly. Throughout her relationships with Tommy and Dale, Libby was not very aware of her own sexual feelings or interests. Although orgasms are certainly not the ultimate yardstick for evaluating sexual fulfillment, Libby spent much of her adult life not even knowing whether she could have one (which of course almost everyone can).

In her sensitive and insightful classic *For Yourself: The Fulfillment of Female Sexuality* (1976), Lonnie Barbach details a step-by-step process by which women can discover the pleasurable sensations inherent in female arousal. For Barbach and many others (for example, Dodson 1987), one key for many women to sexual awareness is masturbation: "Masturbation is one of the best ways to learn about your sexual responses" (Barbach 1976, 88). Barbach proceeds to discuss the historical and social restrictions placed primarily on women which have discouraged them from exploring their sexuality. She concludes that society's aversion to masturbation is ill-founded.

> The guilt, fear, anxiety and repulsion that surrounds masturbation is astounding, especially when one realizes not only how pervasive it is among human beings but how beneficial, pleasurable and relaxing. (88–89)

While presenting a thoughtful and sequential program for helping women achieve sexual fulfillment, Barbach also discusses how important sexual fulfillment can be in one's life:

> Sexual liberation is one aspect of personal liberation. Taking control of your life, at the most intimate, personal, and fundamental level—the level of your sexuality—seems to lead to extending control over other areas of your life. . . . Once we feel better about ourselves, once we assume that we have rights that deserve respect from others, we are in a position to begin liberating ourselves. . . . Liberation means having the freedom to be strong and caring of others, while still being able to be open and accepting of care from others. Liberation entails being free to be passive and receiving or to be assertive and giving. . . . When you can take control of your life and feel free to be yourself, when you are personally liberated, you lose fear. . . . Sexual liberation is a beginning. (197–98)

Moving Beyond Dependency

Probably without knowing the means or outcome, Libby began her personal journey toward sexual and personal satisfaction after Tommy's suicide. With both Dale and John, Libby formed less dependent relationships and began to develop her own sexual identity. Finally, her relationship with Dennis gave her the opportunity to be more her own person, to have orgasms, and to share a mutually satisfying sex life. Her relationship with Dennis awakened her sensual potential and taught her how to be intimate by being aware of her own needs and feelings. Libby is no longer the dependent female who can relate to males only by caring for them. In this, she has overcome her restrictive upbringing to discover new dimensions of herself and her sexuality.

While it is obvious that no single sexual life-style is necessarily the best, Libby's explorations and personal growth have provided a more productive and satisfying life *for her*. Libby is a dynamic woman who had the intelligence, perseverance, and opportunities to create this new sexual life-style for herself. In this, she is most fortunate.

In our next case study, that of Stan Fitzgerald, we will see that developing a satisfying sexual life-style can be quite problematic.

References and Recommended Readings

Barbach, Lonnie. *For Yourself: The Fulfillment of Female Sexuality.* Garden City, N.Y.: Doubleday, 1976.

Dodson, Betty. *Sex for One: The Joy of Selfloving.* New York: Crown, 1987.

Peele, Stanton, and Archie Brodsky. *Love and Addiction.* New York: New American Library, 1975.

Remoff, Heather. *Sexual Choice: A Woman's Decision: Why and How Women Choose the Men They Do as Sexual Partners.* New York: Dutton, 1985.

DISCUSSION AREAS

1. Libby's relationship with Tommy had many features of a marriage made at an early age. What do you see as the strengths and weaknesses of early marriages?

2. Do you think it is necessary to have several lovers and several different significant relationships to learn about one's sexuality as Libby did? Some people have many relationships and yet they never seem to grow or change—why does this happen? Even the trauma of Tommy's suicide eventually served as an impetus for Libby's newly emerging sense of self. How and why did this happen? What events in your life have been pivotal to your growth and maturation?

3. Libby's early family life and her relationship with Tommy encouraged her to be a supportive and dependent female. Do you believe that American society today still promotes this? Are you interested in having a relationship with a dependent person? Why or why not? What type of person would create an optimal relationship with you?

4. Libby reported being attracted to Tommy because he was a jock and good-looking. What role does physical appearance play in your relationship(s)? What role do you think physical appearances should play in a relationship?

5. Which of Libby's sexual involvements seemed to you to be the best? Why? In your view, what constitutes a great relationship?

6. While Libby had a number of sexual relationships, she repeated several times during her interview that she "never had sex just for fun." Do you think recreational sex is wrong? How are sex and intimacy related in your life?

7. Libby began her interview by stating that her romantic and sexual life had not developed in the way she anticipated it would. She found herself involved in situations later in her life which she would not have accepted earlier. Do you think growing older usually tempers one's sexual ideals? Why or why not? Have your sexual ideals changed? If yes, how?

8. Libby thought her affair with Dale (a married man) was justified. Do you agree? Who by category is acceptable or unacceptable to you as a lover? Do categories make any difference to you?

9. Libby described a very sensual massage that she received from Dennis. What is the most sensual experience you have ever had? Is sensuality related to sexuality in your life?

10. Tommy's suicide changed Libby's life forever. How would the death of your lover change you? How are our lives defined by our relationships?

2
Trying to Leave a Traditional Life-style: Case Study of Stan Fitzgerald

tan Fitzgerald, a tall, gaunt, and frail man in his midforties, projects a bohemian, intellectual demeanor, but his sad, recessed eyes reveal much of the personal loneliness he has endured. When Stan looks you squarely in the eye, you can still see traces of youthful promise and idealism, but such revelations from the past are often quickly obscured by a nervous twitch of his head or an anguished cracking of his knuckles.

Stan grew up in the Cajun country and has lived all his life in and around New Orleans. Most of his family still reside in the same neighborhood where he was born. His large, extended, Catholic family includes nearly two hundred people, most of whom Stan still knows on a first-name basis. His father (now deceased) provided a steady, working-class income as a plumber. His mother, a housewife, remains busy with her extended family. His father was quiet and shy, while his mother actively asserted herself within the family. Stan has two brothers, both more than ten years older than he. Stan was not a planned baby. He hardly knew his brothers except as distant role models. Both became plumbers like their father, married early, and live within blocks of Stan's mother, who still lives in the house where Stan was born. Every Sunday after church the members of this extended family still gather for dinner and conversation.

As a child, Stan had many close friends, including a cousin named Ernie, who was his best friend. Ernie and Stan grew up together sharing everything, including rheumatic fever when both were five years old. Stan suffered considerably from the fever and remains frail and sickly to this day. He hated school at first and cried uncontrollably his first day of school; however, he gradually began to enjoy it, and eventually school became the one arena in which he could and did excel.

Early in junior high school, Ernie learned how to masturbate from his older brother. Stan learned from Ernie:

> I was really naive. Ernie told me to "put my hand around my prick this way, and pull up and down," and . . . we would sit in the same room and do it. And we would try to get dirty magazines and things like that. And then I felt guilty. I had a backlash of guilt because of my Catholic upbringing. So, I really tried to

stop. And I abstained from doing that for months at a time. And then I would give in and feel very bad. And my cousin and I used to talk about masturbation and that was a real good release because it made me feel normal. He did it too. And we would compare techniques and whether or not we would tell our wives when we got married, and so on. Ernie also introduced me to the first girl I ever kissed. It was an overwhelming experience. I did it in the bushes behind her mother's house. I just could not handle the feelings. I mean they were not sexual so much, just exciting. I had very romantic ideas about marriage. I really wanted to get married and have a family. And more than anyone else on the block, I was the one who had those ideas. And yet I am the only one, I think, out of the whole group who has not gotten married.

Another important influence on Stan at this time was his older brother, who served more as a role model than as a close friend.

It was like he was a member of the adults and I was the kid. He would side with my parents more often. We never had a sense of being close. Sure, we slept in the same bed, but we did not really know each other. I remember when he got married. I was ten, I think, and I really cried. I missed him. I knew that he was going to leave the house then. And after the time that he was about seventeen and he graduated from high school, his life was really different. I would shine his shoes, and he would give me a quarter or something. He would dress up and go out on a date. You know, I was really interested in what he was doing. But we did not talk anymore. There was such a gap of age, and he did not really tell me about his life because I did not know who he was. I would not have understood, so I was just the little brother. And then he got married and went off. Both of my brothers got married at the age of twenty, so I expected, miraculously, that I would get married at the age of twenty. So I kept waiting, you know, until I was twenty years old. I figured I did not even have to do anything. Then, as soon as I met a girl when I was twenty, I thought, well, this is probably the one. I passively just kept going on, and I was shocked when it did not happen. Well, when I turned twenty-one, God, I thought I was probably going to get a really good one because I had waited a year longer, you know. It sure did not work out that way.

Stan did exceptionally well in high school, particularly in English classes. Life at home was dull, so when he was not out with the neighborhood gang, he read a lot.

During his senior year in high school, several pivotal events occurred. Stan argued constantly with his mother, and he began "hanging out" at a downtown coffeehouse "full of the bohemian intellectual crowd." It was there that he first met people whose intellectual interests aligned with his own. He gave some public readings of his own poetry and began meeting women.

My mom's social view was very tiny, so it really did not relate to the broader perspective of the life I began to know in school and books. Her idea of what was right and wrong was very limited to me, yet I could not convince her otherwise. Arguments with her were never logical. They were emotional and she would over-power me with her emotion. And my father would sit there, and once in a while say, "Aw, leave the kid alone," or something like that. My mother would excel with sarcasm. As I began to become aware of this, I really disliked my home and felt that it was boring.

When I got to high school, I really had this sense of "I have got to get out of this kind of life. I do not want to come home and watch TV every night, go visit the family, and have all these family obligations that take up every bit of my time. There has to be more to life." So in high school, people would meet in coffeehouses, sort of pseudobeatniks, and that was a whole other world. I think all of this was changing my life. I was very studious. I did good work and got good grades, and when I met these people at the coffeehouse, the whole world of art, literature, film, and alternative life-styles opened up to me. And I changed course, because there was excitement there. There were real living people making changes and doing things, and, even as much as I tried, I was still the conservative in that group because I had such an overwhelming backlog from my parents and their restrictions. So I started borrowing my father's car at night, going to the coffeehouse, saying I was going to the library. And I think I turned toward studying and choosing a group of new friends that gave me a chance at some other kind of life.

Stan's chance at some other kind of life took a decidedly sexual turn that same year when he lost his virginity at the local coffeehouse.

The people at the coffeehouse were intelligent, and they were not afraid to talk about anything. They were the smartest people I knew, so my first real sexual experience happened through this coffeehouse. This girl that I really liked decided to initiate me. She grabbed me by the hand and took me upstairs. And there was another couple in this bedroom . . . it was sort of like an orgy party, only not mixed. I mean, everybody coupled off. So I could hear them laughing, and I was trying hard to be cool, and she was very experienced. She had had a really trying childhood and had learned all kinds of things, and she was very pretty to me. I remember she was trying to get me hard and then I took off her panties, and we had sex. I came very fast, which I am sure disappointed her. She left the room to sleep with this older, good-looking guy who was more experienced, and she never came back, which disappointed me. I could hear them making it in the room across the hall, but I still felt good that it had finally happened, and I remember the smell of her juices on my fingers. And I went home Sunday morning, and we had to go to church. And throughout church, I just kept smelling my fingers and at that point decided to give up God and the church and everything. Of course, I did not tell my parents about the girl or my decision right away. I just went through the motions of going to church for a while.

Shortly after this happened, Stan also began to associate less with Ernie and all his other neighborhood friends. Ernie got his high school girlfriend pregnant, so he married her. Stan hated this woman, which increased his separation from Ernie. Ernie also began working in a warehouse where several of his cousins worked. This further divided them, as Stan decided to break the family and neighborhood tradition by going to college. No one in his entire family had ever gone to college. He consciously chose to separate himself in these ways, but these choices created a profound melancholy and loneliness, vestiges of which persist even today.

After high school graduation, Stan lived at home while attending a local college. He continued to socialize with his coffeehouse friends. He began using drugs (marijuana and hallucinogens), for which he was eventually arrested. This arrest underscored his emerging black sheep standing in both his family and his neighborhood.

After I came to college, I stopped going to church. I was raised as a Catholic, and I had to tell my parents that I was not going to church, and that was a heavy number, but I told them in the wake of another event that happened. You know, I had gotten into drugs at the end of my high school days, and as I started college, everything kind of changed. I just did it [took acid] a couple of times, and I got caught in Lake Pontchartrain Park and was arrested and thrown in jail after a whole day of very absurd events.

What happened was, I was tripping [on LSD] and I went for a walk, I found an old lady sitting on her porch and I started singing joyously to her. The old fart called the police. They came and picked me up. The policeman came to arrest me, and I hugged him because he had a pretty blue uniform on, and my eyes were really registering colors. I had an enveloping sense of humor the whole day. I also felt sort of confident, sort of like—well, great. I was just totally innocent and naive, so no one was out to hurt me—they were all charmed. And we went to jail, and even the people in the cells were just laughing along with me and at me sometimes, and telling me stories that I should tell the judge. You know, they were really absurd. I kept doing all this stuff until my father came to the jail because they had called him for me. And he was upset. He was crying, and said, "Oh my God, you are taking dope." There was no distinguishing between different kinds. "It is going to ruin your life. What is going to happen now? I will call a lawyer." And this and that. And I had my mother taking care of a pot plant that they did not even know what it was, and I told them to destroy it, so they were even more frightened. They came with the lawyer the next morning. He was a friend of the family, I guess. But he did not even know my name. He kept getting it wrong, and my age wrong. But there was nothing to it. There was no law against acid at the time. They knew what I had taken, because I just told them. And so they charged me with drunken disturbance, and let me go with a twenty-five-dollar fine. So it was no big thing, but it had a tremendous impact on my family. My oldest brother wanted to disown me. He was talking about how I had ruined the family name and stuff like that. And my mother thought that the devil had possessed me. Nobody could deal with it. My father wanted to take me out of college. My middle brother was actually the most understanding, trying to balance it out because he saw everybody else going crazy.

While Stan's life at home became increasingly complicated, his course work at the local college went well. He eventually graduated with honors and earned a graduate fellowship in literature. Stan's undergraduate sex life always involved women from the coffeehouse in short-term affairs. These affairs invariably ended when the women left Stan. Stan complained that these former lovers always left him for a better-looking man. Somehow his childhood visions of romantic love and an inevitable marriage and family were eluding him.

In graduate school, Stan became sexually involved with Valerie, an attractive young woman who was working as a waitress in a restaurant he frequented. She was divorced and had a four-year-old son. Eventually Valerie, her son, and Stan lived together for several years. During this relationship Stan felt more contented and productive than ever before.

His graduate work went well, which allowed him to finish his Ph.D. and gain a faculty position. Stan was shocked and disappointed when no one from his family would attend his graduation.

Shortly after he finished his degree, Valerie ran off with some "muscular jock type," leaving her son with Stan. Stan, who always enjoyed being around the boy, lovingly looked after him for three years until the boy's father demanded custody.

Stan's involvement with Valerie followed a pattern typical of his intimate relationships with women. Stan sought out unusually attractive women like Valerie, which set him up, for invariably they later ran off with some "jock type."

Stan's sexual relationship with Valerie was problematic. While he found Valerie sexually desirable, he occasionally was impotent with her. Valerie was understanding about these episodes, but he felt this was becoming a serious issue for him.

> The first time I was impotent with Valerie I just entered a state of shock. My shock switched to anger at myself, and then finally shame overcame me. I was so damned embarrassed, I wanted to disappear. Nothing I could do would give me an erection. The more I tried, the softer I became. Valerie was very supportive when she finally realized what was happening, but even her support did not help my overwhelming feeling of helplessness and shame.

Though Stan and Valerie loved each other, they had other sexual issues to confront as well. At Stan's insistence, they had sex only in the missionary position, and Stan preferred to do this in the dark. He did not feel comfortable exploring different sexual techniques. He related with disdain how Valerie had even wanted to make love outdoors one night, an idea he quickly rejected.

Valerie had had other lovers and enjoyed a wide range of sexual activities. Stan felt that her requests to engage in oral sex and other forms of sexual experimentation only made him more uncomfortable and often triggered his impotence. While their sexual problems increased, their ability to communicate openly and share their feelings diminished.

Valerie left, as many of Stan's lovers did, when she wanted to be with somebody else. Predictably, this someone else was more physically appealing than Stan. Being aware of this frustrated Stan. For several years after Valerie left, he continued to live with her son. His work as an assistant professor kept him busy, and he chose to be celibate. During this time Stan re-experienced the melancholy and loneliness that he felt after his first sexual encounter. His feelings of estrangement from his parents and family also re-emerged to haunt him.

I was very lonely and depressed. I guess I was desperate to get over Valerie. Month after month I still wallowed in it. The only rewarding thing was the boy. We shared so much together. I do need kids of my own.

About a year after Valerie's son returned to his father, Stan taught a writing class. In the class he met Connie.

Connie submitted several erotic poems. She was so damn open about sex. It was hard to believe. One essay she wrote was about ménage à trois [sex involving three people]. When I asked the class who would like to read their essay, she immediately volunteered. After she had extolled the virtues of group sex, neither I nor the class knew how to respond. Connie does not filter her comments. She will say anything she feels like saying. Amazing. She was also very aggressive, to which I played disinterested. I sincerely did not want to start sleeping with my students.

Connie, an assertive and dynamic young woman, exudes self-confidence, and her poise complements her great physical beauty. Connie described Stan and their slowly emerging relationship by saying,

Stan is very sensitive. He feels life. He also is a genius who can provoke you intellectually. I know this sounds corny, but I first saw him as a sort of god who knew it all. I was shocked to find out how uptight he is. He is tense, and he worries constantly. In bed it is almost like he is afraid to let go and enjoy himself. I think I frightened him sexually.

Stan and Connie began seeing each other socially. Connie first asked Stan out to a play. Thereafter, they attended various parties and cultural events without becoming sexually intimate. During this time a transformation began.

We went out together three or four nights a week. After a couple of months Connie was no longer just a bright student. She became a person in her own right and finally a desirable woman.

After dating each other for almost three months, Stan and Connie became lovers, which created an important new bond between them. At this stage in their relationship, Connie was still in awe of him. A few months later Connie decided she loved Stan and wanted more commitment in their relationship. She asked him to move in with her as a first step toward getting married. Having known Connie for only about six months, Stan felt her offer was premature and that they did not need to get "that serious." While she accepted his evaluation and continued seeing him, this confrontation marked the beginning of her serious doubts about their relationship. At this time, she also recalled starting to have serious doubts about what they called Stan's "uptightness." Stan's uptightness, or impotence, initially happened only occasionally. While Connie said this did not really bother her, Stan found these incidents increasingly depressing.

For the next six months their relationship remained basically satisfying to both. Stan felt that her companionship and social poise made his life interesting. Connie valued him as a supportive friend and knowledgeable teacher who had taught her "more than anyone else." During this period, he became increasingly committed to her, while she became less eager to build a long-term relationship.

After another year, Connie began having serious questions about Stan and their future together. She reported that he liked "stiff academic parties" while she liked "to boogie." She loved outdoor and athletic activities while he preferred chess or reading. These differences between them which once seemed intriguing now began to seem damaging. Connie asked Stan if he thought they should start dating other people. He replied, "No." She reported feeling the need for more time alone, while he reported that their sex life began to deteriorate still further. Although they rarely discussed their sexual sharing, he wanted more sexual contact while she wanted less. Ironically, while he wanted more sexual contact, he also became impotent more often.

> We still slept together several nights a week, but sexual contact almost stopped. Connie would come over real late and I would already be asleep or else she would be tired, or not in the mood, or something else would intervene. It was always something. Looking back, I can see that she was unconsciously backing away, and our sex life reflected it.

Stan and Connie began arguing over events both felt were trivial. They started seeing each other less. Connie also told Stan she was going to start "seeing other men." Shortly after this announcement, Stan's father suffered a serious heart attack. Stan returned home, where his father asked him when he was going to "settle down and start a family." (His two older brothers were long married, and both had several children.) Although still something of an outcast at home, Stan felt strong emotional ties to his family. His father's questions triggered an awareness that he did want to start a family.

Within a week, his father died. Reeling emotionally, Stan went to Connie proposing marriage. Arriving at Connie's apartment, Stan found her cooking dinner for another man. Ignoring the upcoming dinner, he proposed. She assured him that she cared for him, but now she did not want that commitment. When Connie's date arrived, Stan became quite angry and swore they were finished.

Since that night, they have not seen or spoken to one another. He continues to be angry and hurt, maintaining that she is "too flighty and immature to make a serious commitment to anyone or anything." According to him, she just wants "to play around with jocks."

Stan, now forty-five, enjoys being a tenured professor but dislikes being uninvolved, celibate, and lonely. He spends much time reminiscing about Connie, particularly about her early interest in getting married. He steadfastly maintains that Connie would make an excellent mother for his children.

Connie is sexually involved with several men who are noticeably younger and more attractive than Stan. When interviewed, Connie reported that she hardly ever thinks about Stan anymore. She remains convinced that she never wants to be a mother or raise children.

ANALYSIS

Stan's case is dramatically different from that of Libby Williams. In many ways the two are polar opposites. Libby embraced a traditional and dependent marriage only to discover that she needed something different. Stan fairly quickly rejected his family's traditional social/sexual life-style only to discover that his idealized relationship and family were most elusive. Libby ultimately achieved a satisfying sexual life-style; Stan has not.

Impotence

Sexually, Stan suffers from what Masters and Johnson term secondary impotence:

> If a man is to be judged secondarily impotent, there must be the clinical landmark of at least one instance of successful intromission, either during the initial coital opportunity or in a later episode. The usual pattern of the secondarily impotent male is success with the initial coital opportunity and continual effective performance with the first fifty, hundred or even thousand or more coital encounters. Finally, an episode of failure at effective coital connection is recorded. (Masters and Johnson 1970, 149)

They go on to describe how this initial coital failure often becomes repeated, generating performance anxieties and more coital failures involving either erection problems or ejaculation problems, or both. Secondary impotence is almost always associated with psychological or social stress and is not physiologically based. Secondary impotence almost always can be eliminated with effective therapy. Masters and Johnson report a 73.8 percent success rate in relieving secondary impotence during their short, two-week residential clinical program (1970, 204).

The key to relieving secondary impotence is to create opportunities to think and feel sexual without specific pressures to perform. Part of the Masters and Johnson therapeutic approach to secondary impotence is to ban coital contact for a while while partners instead engage in a wide array of sensual touching and sharing exercises.

It is obvious that Stan's uptightness, as he describes it, perpetuates his performance anxieties and impotence. If Stan wanted to deal with his impotence, he could certainly seek out competent professional therapy, or he could try one of the readily available therapeutic guidebooks.

Self-help Books

Harvey Gochros and Joel Fischer's book *Treat Yourself to a Better Sex Life* (1980) offers many practical approaches for achieving sexual enhancement. One of the first issues they deal with is the common sexual myths. Some of the myths that may be complicating Stan's sexual relationships include the following:

> Sex is essentially intercourse.
>
> There is only one right way to have sex.
>
> Both partners should have orgasms every time they have sexual contact.
>
> A large penis is essential to arouse and satisfy a woman.
>
> If your sex life is healthy you should not have to masturbate.
>
> If you really loved me I would not have to tell you what I like sexually.
>
> True love makes you a mind reader. (Grochros and Fischer 1980, 14–25, 135–37)

Good communication, a common desire to share sexual pleasure, and a willingness to find a mutually satisfying sexual life seem essential to creating a healthy sexual relationship. Stan has serious problems in all three areas.

Value Clarification

In addition, Stan would probably benefit from some personal value clarification, as well as techniques to build up his own self-esteem and confidence. In his book *Getting Unstuck: Breaking Through Your Barriers to Change* (1988), Sidney Simon provides a practical and clear game plan for personal change. Most noted for his work on value clarification, Simon suggests that before change can occur a person has to decide what his or her priorities really are. In Stan's case it is not clear what he really wants. He says he wants to be involved with dynamic, independent women, and yet on another level he seems to insist on exclusively asserting his own wishes, sexually and otherwise. He also speaks often of his desire for a family, and yet he became involved with women who had little interest in being mothers (Valerie and Connie). Stan would probably benefit from Simon's approach to value clarification (see Simon 1988, 115–45).

As Stan seeks value clarification, he needs to be realistic. As we grow older, we should become able to temper our idealism with a growing sense of what is really feasible. Stan needs to be realistic in determining what type of woman would be satisfying to him in a long-term relationship. This decision should be influenced by a realistic appraisal of what he really can and cannot provide in a relationship. For example, if Stan becomes certain that he wants to be involved with a dynamic, innovative woman, then he will probably have to be willing to try some of the experimental sexual activities that he so quickly rejected with Connie.

Sexual Self-esteem

Stan has many doubts about himself and his ability to retain lovers. Throughout his interview, he constantly talked about how the women he had known chose to run off with some better-looking or more athletic guy. Simon has specific suggestions on how to increase self-esteem while blocking destructive self-fulfilling prophecies. Simon suggests that mentors and role models can be used to inspire, encourage, and give hope about doing better. One should also muster the courage to take more risks, developing more emotional support by cultivating a group of supportive friends. More personal power can be developed by being more decisive and assertive, while still being sensitive and receptive to the needs of others. Simon also suggests that an individual identify and use his or her own unique qualities while looking for new ways and places to belong. Finally, he asserts that one can identify projects or tasks that can reasonably be accomplished, thereby gaining a sense of achievement (1988, 60–84).

   Although it is always easier to criticize the lives of others, I think it is important not to write off Stan and his problems. Since we generally treat our intimate relationships so privately, many individuals suffer from sexual problems that they feel they cannot even discuss. In this regard, Stan is at least willing to discuss his problems. It is not clear whether Stan will ever be able to resolve the dilemmas he faces, sexually, emotionally, and socially. One can only hope that he finds the courage to try.

   Our next case study reviews the life of Nick Orren. Nick did a lot of sexual experimenting in a variety of different relationships. Through these relationships he resolved many conflicts between his idealized romantic life and what was intrinsically satisfying. Nick Orren launched a more successful quest to find a satisfying sexual life.

References and Suggested Readings

Gochros, Harvey, and Joel Fischer. *Treat Yourself to a Better Sex Life*. Englewood Cliffs, N.J.: Prentice Hall, 1980.

Masters, William, and Virginia Johnson. *Human Sexual Inadequacy*. New York: Bantam, 1970.

Simon, Sidney B. *Getting Unstuck: Breaking Through Your Barriers to Change.* New York: Warner Books, 1988.

Zilbergeld, Bernie. *Male Sexuality: A Guide to Sexual Fulfillment.* New York: Bantam, 1984.

DISCUSSION AREAS

1. Stan has not developed satisfying romantic and sexual relationships. Why do you think this happened? Why do you think Stan's lovers invariably leave him?

2. Stan does not want the traditional life-style of his Catholic family. Professionally, he has not suffered from this, but it has certainly complicated his romantic involvements. How can he find satisfaction in an intimate relationship?

3. The coffeehouse society offered a new social world for Stan. Women at the coffeehouse were bright and independent, which Stan found exciting. How have women of this type complicated Stan's life? Do you think his ideals for a girlfriend are actually practical for him? Have your ideals for a lover worked out well?

4. Stan has always been interested in extremely attractive women, while he himself is not a physically impressive person. Society postulates that in most instances, relationships have some kind of balance in terms of physical appearance. Indeed, when this balance is violated, questions are asked. If an old, unattractive male is seen in a romantic setting with a young and attractive female, often certain questions are asked and certain assumptions are made. Do you think Stan is setting himself up to lose by picking women who are physically attractive while he himself is rather plain? How does physical appearance affect your relationships?

5. Stan found it satisfying to be a stepfather to Valerie's son. Why do you think Stan found stepparenting so easy and enjoyable? Do you see children as complicating or enriching your relationships? Many people like Connie see no procreative future for themselves. For you, how are the issues of sex and procreation related?

6. Stan has had a fairly long series of unpleasant sexual relationships. Even his first sexual relationship ended rather abruptly when his lover left to sleep with another man. Stan does not have a good sexual self-image. All of this is related to and compounded by his occasional impotence. Do you think Stan's impotence is a major problem? How could Stan strengthen his sense of sexual identity and find a sexual relationship that is more satisfying to him? How much do you think your identity affects your sexuality? How have you or would you deal with the issue of impotence? How does your sexuality affect your self-image?

7. Stan, like many of us, experiences a kind of dialectic tension between his idealized relationships and reality. In rejecting his traditional Catholic upbringing, he decided that ideally he would like to be in-

volved with an independent woman, yet involvements with this type of woman have been problematic for him. In your opinion, can Stan resolve this dialectic tension? How do you deal with the difference between your romantic ideal and the actual people with whom you have become involved? Stan describes himself as a romantic, and yet his life has hardly been very romantic. How do you explain that? If you were speaking to Stan as a friend, what advice would you give him?

8. In retrospect, Stan stated that he should have moved in with Connie when she wanted that commitment as a precursor to marriage. The question here is one of timing a commitment so that both partners have relatively equal interests. Do you think Stan and Connie would be happily married now if he had been less cautious about moving in with her? How have timing and reciprocity of commitment affected your sexual relationships?

9. Connie wanted to share a wide variety of sexual techniques and experiences with Stan while he wanted a fairly conservative and restricted sex life with her. How should couples resolve these kinds of differences? Have you dealt with these kinds of different preferences?

10. What single event in your life has done the most to enhance your sexual self-identity? What event damaged your sexual self-identity the most?

3
Sexual Experimentation Leading Finally to a More Traditional Relationship: Case Study of Nick Orren

Nick Orren, a tall, large man in his forties, projects his confidence and relaxed manner through his infectious smile and sense of humor. He likes being around people and has been known to tell a tale or two. His open and expressive personality facilitated a straightforward discussion of his sexual development.

Born in Santa Monica, California, shortly after World War II, Nick was the younger brother in an increasingly prosperous family. His older brother, Ray, the family's superachiever, distinguished himself both athletically and academically.

Nick's parents maintained a loving relationship sprinkled with periodic and predictable quarrels. His father, who was well educated, eventually became a successful land developer. Nick's father had been athletic his whole life and sexually independent. Although he was affectionate toward Nick's mother and maintained an ongoing love for her, it was no secret within the family that the father from time to time had discreet affairs. Nick's mom believed that "men need to sow some wild oats." Nick identified more with his father than with his mother. His father, an athletic, successful, and charismatic figure who exuded great self-confidence, also had an imposing physical presence and personal charm, which made him very comfortable around women. This was something Nick was to inherit.

Nick's first sexual memory involved visiting his three male cousins.

I remember playing one afternoon with my three cousins over in one of their neighbors' garages. I must have been about seven years old, and my cousins were a couple of years older than I was. They asked me if I had any money with me at the time. I think I had a dollar or two. They told me to give them the money because I was about to get a real treat. We went into this neighbor's garage, and they gave a bunch of money, including mine, to an older girl. Then my older cousins and I sort of sat down in this garage and waited. Several girls, probably between ten and twelve, came in and started doing a striptease act. I remember that my older cousins thought this was great fun. And while I did think it was fun, I am not sure that I saw the point. I had seen my mother naked around the house. Nudity was not that big an issue, but the way the young girls twisted and turned their bodies, it was obvious that they felt they were giving us a treat, and it was also obvious from my cousins' behavior that they too considered this a major treat. I remember this as my first sexual experience because this mild striptease was really my first glimpse into the world of playful, naughty sex.

Nick also recalled two experiences that he had in the sixth grade. First, he learned about sex from his friends on the school soccer team. One day his soccer buddies told him that men put their penises into women and then babies start growing. He remembered that this seemed sort of strange, neither frightening nor pleasing. It all seemed rather abstract.

This abstractness was compounded later in sixth grade during a sex education class when a short film was shown with cartoon characters called Johnny Sperm and Susie Egg. Johnny Sperm and Susie Egg got together and babies were made. The filmstrip showed no human physiology other than the cartoon characters depicting sperm and eggs. After the film, Nick's father asked him if he had any other questions about sex. Nick, being too embarrassed to pursue it with his father, felt that at least he understood the basics.

In junior high school Nick became a good gymnast, traveling with the gymnastics team around the state to various competitive events. On one of these trips, several of the older boys gathered at the back of the bus to discuss masturbation. Talking in hushed voices, they assured Nick that, being only twelve, he was too young to know about this. However, he persevered, and they explained how they had been masturbating. Nick, having recently undergone puberty himself, decided to try this. He began masturbating regularly and has never abandoned the habit.

Also in junior high Nick taught his cousin, Carl, to masturbate. The two boys slept together when Carl arrived for a weekend visit. The first night Nick asked Carl if he knew about masturbating. Although slightly older than Nick, Carl knew nothing about the subject. Nick showed Carl how to masturbate and then actually masturbated him. Initially, Carl felt that it hurt, but when he had an orgasm, he found the experience both frightening and pleasurable.

Nick said he never felt guilty about his masturbation experiences, even though one day his brother, Ray, saw him doing it. Embarrassed by Nick's masturbating, Ray quickly walked out of the room. The next day Nick's father talked to him about masturbating. His father said that he did not feel it did any harm, although eventually Nick would find out that the pleasures of being with a woman far exceeded those of masturbation. The only word of caution that Nick's father gave him about masturbating was to be sure not to let his mother see him doing it.

In junior high, Nick identified with the athletes, and while he did attend school dances, his social life clearly revolved around boys rather than girls. Toward the end of Nick's junior high school years, his family became wealthy and moved to Pacific Palisades. Nick began attending an elite private high school.

In that school, Nick's social relationships began to change. While doing well athletically and academically, he also began dating on a regular basis. Though he experienced some initial awkwardness and embarrassment in asking girls out, he quickly discovered that since he was an attractive, athletic male whose family had good social standing, many girls, including some of the most popular, were eager to go out with him. Nick dated several girls in high school, but by the end of his junior year he began "going steady" with one named Anna. Anna, a runner-up for junior prom queen, a class officer, and a leader in the pep squad, was generally considered a real catch, particularly by the members of Nick's gymnastic team.

Anna and I dated steadily for a year and a half, as I finished high school. I must confess that in hindsight I think I dated her for all of the wrong reasons. We were somewhat friendly with each other, but I do not think I really liked her as a person. She was not a sensitive person, not a giving person, and she always remained aloof emotionally. She was a bit of a snob. I think the reason I dated her was because she was the kind of girl that all of my friends thought they wanted to date. I dated her almost exclusively for social impact.

Nick never had sex with Anna, but they would go "parking." Nick's family by this time had money so he had access to fancy cars. After borrowing one of his father's new cars, they would go out parking and do some "heavy petting." This involved his masturbating her and engaging in some French-kissing. She in turn would masturbate him by rubbing his groin outside his pants without putting her hands in his pants. This utilitarian and socially convenient relationship seemed satisfactory to both until the evening of their senior prom. Nick's father was suddenly called out of town, and his mother did not want to let Nick drive one of the new cars. So Nick picked up Anna in his own car, an older and not particularly fashionable one. Anna began crying immediately because she felt it just would not do to arrive at the senior prom in Nick's own car. After this incident Nick never took her out again.

The summer before he began college, Nick visited an old gymnastics

friend, Ents, who had been an older member of Nick's high school gymnastics team. Ents was good-looking and confident, and now attended
college, where he lived with his girlfriend. Nick remembers well the weekend he spent with his old friend:

> I visited Ents and his girlfriend one weekend and stayed in their
> apartment. They were affectionate and loving. His girlfriend was
> very attractive, and I must confess I found her sexually alluring.
> She enjoyed having me around and, I think, enjoyed sexually
> teasing me a little bit. At one point, she even asked me if I had
> slept with Anna. One night after I had gone to bed, Ents and his
> girlfriend began making love on the living room couch. I came
> out of my bedroom and saw them making love. I watched for
> some time thinking they would not see me. I must confess, I found
> it exciting and erotic. The next day, much to my embarrassment,
> I found out that Ents had seen me watching. He did not make a
> big deal of it—he just laughed it off—and in some way, I con-
> sidered his relaxed, confident, and loving sexual style to be the
> very model of what I hoped to achieve!

During his freshman year at college Nick met Kristin and she physically reminded him a great deal of his mother, whom he always considered attractive. Kristin was tall and thin, like his mother, and even spoke
in the same gentle manner. Kristin and Nick began spending lots of time
together. At first they were just friends. Kristin liked working out on the
gymnastic equipment, and she had a naturally pleasant outlook. She loved
the outdoors, and although Nick enjoyed the outdoors, he had never spent
as much time in it as she had. They went backpacking, visited on the
beach, and slowly developed a powerful romantic attachment. Ultimately,
Nick, in a rather formal, verbal way, asked Kristin if she would be willing
to have sex with him.

> I will never forget that first night with Kristin. Looking back, it
> has to be rather funny, but at the time it certainly did not seem
> so. While Kristin and I had never really discussed our previous
> sexual experiences, I did know that she had never had sex with
> anyone. She, for some reason, assumed that I was more experi-
> enced sexually than I was. She had a fear of pregnancy, and so I
> had purchased condoms. I put one of these on, but she was not
> sure one was enough; I ended up wearing a second one. All of
> these logistics rather diminished the spontaneity and passion of
> the moment, and when we began to try to make love it was
> painful for her. Ultimately, that night we never did make love.

She had begun bleeding. My initial excitement was severely diminished. That first evening was just a disaster.

Nick and Kristin eventually began making love on a regular basis. Kristin decided that the pill was not an excessive risk for her, and Nick enjoyed giving up the condoms. Their friendship and romantic relationship lasted all through his freshman year and well into his sophomore year at college.

In the middle of Nick's sophomore year, Kristin's father became very ill, so she returned home to help care for him. Since she lived a considerable distance from the college, this meant that for weeks on end she was unable to see Nick. Nick, who reported being "very much in love with her," found this long separation painful and lonely.

One night at a party, Nick met Laura and while he was somewhat drunk took her home and had sex with her. He said that he had used the alcohol as an excuse for betraying Kristin. He also admitted that "part of him" definitely wanted to have sex with Laura and maybe even a relationship.

When he told Kristin about Laura, she became most upset. Her father was getting better by then, so she returned to school. With Kristin's return, Nick said he was willing to end his new relationship with Laura. However, during the turmoil over Laura, Nick began planning a Christmas vacation to Mexico. Several of his gymnastics buddies were going, all with girlfriends, so it seemed essential to have a partner. Kristin, now unsure of her commitment to Nick, decided at the last minute not to go. Angry and disappointed, Nick invited Laura, who accepted. The two-week trip to Mexico aroused new passions in Nick, and by the time they returned from Mexico he was very much in love with Laura.

Laura opened up new sexual worlds to Nick. Laura's family had money, and during her extensive travels she had had innumerable sexual relationships. Her family owned an island in the Caribbean which Laura and Nick visited several times. Being exceptionally bright, Laura attended the university on a full academic scholarship. She was uninhibited, passionate, witty, and highly opinionated; she also believed passionate sex should occur anytime, anywhere, and in any configuration. Nick's sexual experiences with Kristin had been relatively limited. While reflecting on his relationship with Kristin, Nick was not sure Kristin had ever had an orgasm. Unlike Kristin, Laura was sexually assertive, and their new sex life together included oral and anal activities.

The summer after their junior year in college, Nick and Laura decided to live together. Laura rented a palatial house for the two of them to share. Nick said that the following experience was typical of his relationship with Laura:

I remember we moved into the new house for the summer, and the first night Laura, who was an excellent cook, fixed a wonderful dinner for us both. Then she insisted on having sex on top of the dining room table in our new dining room. Afterwards, meals in that room were always special.

Because Laura was wealthy and they pooled their financial resources, Nick no longer had to work. Instead, he traveled extensively with Laura. They would go to New York for weekend parties or up to the Cape to visit her family. But Laura was not only very passionate but also highly opinionated. Their relationship finally revolved around either "arguing or screwing."

When Nick and Laura graduated later that year, Laura decided it would be best to separate. Through her family's connections, Laura took a prestigious and high-paying job in Europe. Nick had never been jilted before, and he found himself trying to decide what to do next. Separating from Laura and moving out of their house, he found himself socially adrift with a fresh undergraduate degree in political science. The degree in political science was undertaken largely to please his father, who had hoped Nick would go on to law school and then join the family development corporation. Nick felt that in some fundamental way, his degree, his family's country club life-style, and Laura were all part of the same problem.

What did he want to do with the rest of his life? He decided to travel for the next several months. He visited college friends from across the country, also spending a little time in Canada. Upon returning to Los Angeles, he started part-time volunteer work at a neighborhood free clinic. While working at the free clinic, Nick moved into a new social world of young volunteers and professional people who were committed to the idea of helping create a more humanistic community. Though the clinic was underfunded, it provided critically needed services to the neighborhood. The clinic staff took pride in helping meet the community's health care needs.

Nick first became sexually involved with one of the women who had recruited him to work in the clinic. Since she was not interested in having a long-term affair with him, he quickly found himself sexually involved in a serial way with several women who worked at the clinic. These relationships were more like good friendships with sex added. Though Nick was keen on finding another significant relationship, most of the women involved in this clinic-based social network seemed to prefer casual, laissez-faire relationships.

Eventually Nick met Rita, who worked as an administrative assistant for the clinic, and they began a relationship that lasted several years. Rita was different from other women Nick had known in that she was more than ten years older, plain looking, poor, and had children from two previous relationships (one in which she was married, the second in which she was not); she also combined a spontaneous love of life with a blithe indifference toward the future. Sexually, Rita felt Nick was "pretty damned naive." Co-opting Marxist terminology, Rita often accused Nick of having a "bourgeois consciousness and life-style." She liked using drugs: marijuana, cocaine, and hallucinogenic drugs such as psilocybin and LSD. Although Nick had tried marijuana, he had not sampled these other drugs. During the time he spent with Rita they tried all of these drugs, and group sex as well.

Rita and I lived in the loft of a large house which was owned by one of the major donors to the clinic. He was kind of a crazy guy who threw lots of casual dinners and parties. The house seemed to always be full of people who were community conscious and supporting the work of the clinic. But there were also lots of their friends passing through town, people visiting, and quite frankly there was just a lot of sleeping around. One night, shortly after one of these elaborate dinners with probably twenty of us eating a huge meal of couscous, one of Rita's best friends from the East Coast arrived for a visit. The house was full of people, and it was obvious that Rita's friend should stay in the apartment with us. Rita's friend had just separated from her husband of many years; she was feeling lonely and isolated. She also found the social atmosphere at the house somewhat strange. Rita's friend was clever, witty, and extremely good-looking, and I must admit that even initially I was sexually attracted to her.

I went to bed that night and Rita came in probably a half hour after I was asleep. She told me that her friend was lonely and was probably still sexually hung up on her ex-husband. I did not see what that really had to do with us. Rita got a strange twinkle in her eye and said what her friend probably needed was to be involved in a new and loving relationship. Rita had had a lesbian affair or two. She suggested that her friend come to bed with us that night. I was rather surprised by the idea and a bit shocked, but I could see that Rita was excited about this. I was both curious and nervous, myself. The three of us spent that night together caressing, touching, making love to each other. Sometimes the women would be involved with each other and I would just watch. Sometimes I would be involved with the other woman, sometimes with Rita. I must confess, I think we spent that whole first night caressing, touching, and having sex.

The next day at the clinic I was totally wasted. We continued to share a sexual relationship between all three of us for the next month or so. All of us felt a little naughty and adventurous doing this. I guess it was sort of like a lark, but later on I found myself wanting to have more time alone with Rita. It was Rita I cared about. Ultimately, this was not emotionally satisfying to Rita's friend, so she became involved with another man and eventually moved in with him.

Nick reported that he not only loved Rita but enjoyed being with her because she had a playful, carefree attitude about life. However, he did not find Rita particularly attractive, and he was alarmed that she had no plans for the future. Her indifference to the future, which upset Nick, was complicated when she discovered she was pregnant. Though she had been using birth control pills, she occasionally forgot one. She claimed indifference about keeping or aborting the fetus. She really wanted Nick to make a commitment to her and the new child or else admit his lack of commitment. Nick suspected Rita was trying to use the child to secure a long-term commitment at precisely the time when he was having serious doubts about their relationship. Since she professed indifference, Nick suggested that she have an abortion. She agreed. Nick stayed with her during the operation but afterward the closeness they had shared was gone. While Rita had taught him much about life, Nick now wanted to do something more productive with his life. He decided to return to graduate school in English literature.

While pursuing a demanding graduate program, Nick wanted a significant and stable, long-term relationship. Back from her prestigious job in Europe, Laura had returned to the United States seeking new horizons. Since she and Nick had remained in contact following their separation, they decided to try living together again.

Laura and I rented a great apartment together and tried to see if we could rekindle the passions that had brought us together in the first place. Indeed, we discovered that we still loved each other, and our sex was very passionate. However, there continued to be severe interpersonal problems. Laura, from my viewpoint, seemed determined to wear the pants. She wanted to make all the decisions, and every issue in our life together was a struggle over who would decide. We seemed to have a constant power battle between us. I think, in many ways, we were just the wrong personality types for each other. Laura eventually married a supportive but unassertive male. I have since visited them several times, and I am convinced that he was the very type she needed.

After Laura left, Nick spent almost six months sexually uninvolved. He spent a lot of time studying and teaching. He found he relished his new professional life, but interpersonally and sexually he felt lonely.

Vivid fantasies and masturbation were poor substitutes for a passionate relationship.

That summer at the Aspen Colorado Music Festival he met Marie. An attractive young woman, Marie lacked self-confidence but had a gentle, caring, and supportive manner. Marie and Nick became friends at the festival, and initially nothing romantic happened between them. Nick enjoyed their friendship but did not feel sexually attracted to Marie.

He returned to graduate school while she shortly thereafter accepted a governess position in Beverly Hills. Over the next two or three months they began spending more time with each other. Eventually the relationship turned sexual. Finally, she moved into his apartment. They lived together for the next six years, while he finished his graduate work. They had a kind and caring relationship with an intense but predictable sex life. They both reported that their relationship was what they needed at that stage in their lives. Nick found his graduate studies intellectually challenging, which complemented his stable relationship with Marie. She, on the other hand, liked the support and confidence he placed in her and began to develop new professional interests. They bought a house together; this was a comfortable, sustaining relationship for them both. Nick believed there was a tacit understanding they would probably get married and have children someday.

As Nick finished his graduate degree, Marie began to sense, with newfound confidence in herself, that she wanted new adventures, new challenges. Since she had never had a positive sexual relationship except with Nick, she decided to become involved with other men. Unilaterally, she moved out. This crushed Nick, and when she left he was devastated. His whole world was in transition again. He felt he was getting too old to start over again on the dating scene.

Nick began his new job as an assistant professor and for the next year had a series of casual sexual involvements. None of them seemed significant to him. He was searching for someone special, someone with whom he could have a family.

> I think this period in my life was definitely my most promiscuous. I did not really want it to be that way—it just sort of worked out that way. I was involved with a number of women. Each of them seemed to have dimensions to their personalities which I found interesting but none of them, overall, seemed that powerful. I am not trying to brag or make myself out as any sexual Adonis, but one day, rather unintentionally, I ended up having sex with four different women. I am not particularly proud of this kind of behavior, but I think there is a common myth that sex is scarce—that most men probably want a lot more sex than they can actually have. I think this is bogus. There is a lot of sex

available. I think the significant issue is the quality of the sexual relationship, not the quantity.

During his second year as an assistant professor, Nick was invited over to a friend's house for dinner. At that dinner, he met Dana, a woman he found to be most interesting. The evening was spent in playful sparring over one issue or another, and he was impressed by this woman's quick repartee, her cosmopolitan outlook, and her knowledge about social situations and people in general. Although he did not see her for several weeks, he began thinking about her. Eventually they arranged to meet again. She seemed rather aloof at the time as she had a number of ongoing sexual relationships. She too was looking for someone special with whom she could share her life. After spending most of that first date talking to each other, they discovered they had a special kind of intensity together.

Dana is a remarkable woman. I cannot think of any other way to describe her. She has traveled all over the world and has acquired the sophistication which travel sometimes brings. She is attractive, bright, lively, and she is her own woman without being obnoxiously assertive like Laura. We found we had a lot in common and that we enjoyed being with each other a great deal. We developed an outstanding friendship. Neither of us was in any rush to make this relationship into a big deal. We both had had lots of involvements, had learned and been pained through those involvements. I remember a D.H. Lawrence line about "old battered warriors." While we were not all that old (we were in our midthirties), I felt like we had both been through quite a bit. But even from its initial onset, I think it had a special intensity. Overall, if I could single out one quality about it, it was that we felt so at ease with each other. She was the kind of person who could inspire me but at the same time accept who I was. We see a lot of issues differently, but usually we can still be there for each other.

Sexually, our relationship has gone through a number of phases. At first we had that dynamic intensity that many new relationships have. I think we have had periods where sex was good but certainly not great, and then invariably we find ways to renew our sexual energy and we move into an intense phase again. Dana really does embody the kind of woman I had always hoped I would love. We eventually decided we wanted to get married, particularly because we wanted to have children together. We now have a boy and a girl, and I must confess that while externally this looks like a very traditional marriage, I am pleased with it. I have seen too many relationships crumble to be certain that our relationship will last forever, but I do know that it is the most dynamic and most secure relationship I have ever been in. We are both committed to trying to spend the rest of our lives together. It is wonderful to have children. They add a whole new dimension to our relationship. They demand more and give more than I ever expected. We have been married monogamously some ten years now, and again, while we go through peaks and valleys, I am hopeful that this relationship will remain as the cornerstone of my life. I do love her!

In conclusion, Nick expressed his belief that most of his varied sexual experiences helped him grow and achieve the kind of maturity and perspective necessary to build his relationship with Dana. Nick feels that people who get married early often have not had many opportunities to find out who they want to become. While this process of growth certainly continues throughout life, Nick felt it was extremely valuable for him to have been involved with these different women so that he could discover what kind of relationship worked best for him.

ANALYSIS

Nick Orren has had a varied sexual life and has been involved with a number of lovers in relationships ranging from single, transitory sexual encounters to long-term monogamous ones. Since he has been sexually involved with this variety of partners and activities, what do we make of his case?

Life Structures

Daniel Levinson and associates have written a ground-breaking book on the developmental periods of adult men. In *The Seasons of a Man's Life,* they studied life structures and the evolution of those structures, to discover an underlying pattern.

> By "life structure" we mean the underlying pattern or design of a person's life at a given time. Here we are studying the lives of men. A man's life has many components: his occupation, his love relationships, his marriage and family, his relation to himself, his use of solitude, his roles in various social contexts—all the relationships with individuals, groups and institutions that have significance to him . . . By studying all of these components we see that they form a basic source of order in the life cycle. The order exists at an underlying level. At the more immediate day-to-day level of concrete action, events and experiences, our lives are often rapidly changing and fragmented. (Levinson et al. 1978, 41)

Levinson and associates go on to state that while every life is idiosyncratic and varied, there usually is an underlying developmental pattern that provides shape and meaning to the individual through his life structure. These researchers contend that focusing exclusively on any single component of an individual's development often means that this underlying developmental structure is not understood or even identified. They describe five significant components they believe are essential in understanding a given individual's life structure: forming and modifying a dream, forming and modifying an occupation, love-marriage-family, forming mentoring relationships, and forming mutual friendships.

Sexuality as a Developmental Process

In analyzing the sexual life of Nick Orren, what are the significant dimensions of his life structure? Since Levinson and associates did not emphasize sexuality in their research, let us use their investigative format and combine it with a developmental sexuality sequence used by Harvey Fierstein. In several of his plays about relationships and sexuality, Fierstein (1978, 1988) describes three fairly distinct phases in sexual development.

First is the self-focused stage in which one becomes sexually aware and involved but remains somewhat emotionally isolated and self-absorbed. Nick's relationships with Anna and Kristin typify this developmental phase. About dating Anna, Nick even said, "I do not think I really liked her as a person." With Kristin even coital logistics were complicated by poor communication and a lack of empathy. Sexually, Nick was not even sure Kristin ever had an orgasm, although "she might have." In terms of mentors and friends, Nick's statements about Ents were revealing. Though he admired Ents's relationship, with its good communication and emotional intimacy, Nick could not establish one for himself. During this first phase Nick's professional future was as unfocused as his ability to be emotionally intimate.

Harvey Fierstein's second developmental stage focuses on the issue of being a couple. In this stage, the involved lovers work out how they will function both as a couple and as individuals. This process can become quite complicated and intellectually convoluted.

R.D. Laing, in his book of poems called *Knots,* provides many painful examples of this.

How can she be happy when the man she loves is unhappy
He feels she is blackmailing him by making him feel
    guilty
    because she is unhappy that he is unhappy
She feels he is trying to destroy her love for him by
    accusing her of being selfish when the trouble is that
    she can't be so selfish as to be happy when the man
    she loves is unhappy
She feels that there must be something wrong with
    her to love someone who can be so cruel as to destroy
    her love for him and is too guilty to be happy, and
    instead is unhappy because he is guilty
He feels that he is unhappy because he is guilty
    to be happy when others are unhappy and that he made
    a mistake to marry someone who can only think of
    happiness.[1] (Laing 1970, 28)

In this second stage of defining what it means to be a couple, many issues need to be explored and resolved if the relationship is going to

---

[1]From *Knots* by R.D. Laing, p.28. © 1970 by R.D. Laing. Published by Pantheon Books, A Division of Random House, Inc. Reprinted with permission.

survive and prosper. Nick's relationships with both Laura and Rita involved many of the developmental issues typical of this second stage. With Laura there were continuous emotional confrontations like the ones described by Laing. Nick reported that while Laura "opened up whole new worlds sexually," they constantly fought over how to be a couple. With Rita, Nick began to question his career goals and life-style. In that relationship what it meant to be a couple even got linked to issues of "bourgeois consciousness" and what collectively they wanted to do in the community. Even the group sex experience helped them explore the parameters of their relationship.

Alex Comfort provides this analysis of a group sex scene at Sandstone, California, available only to heterosexual couples:

> The idea of a wholly open sexual scene [for group sex] is so fantasy loaded, in our culture, and generally mindblowing that it's difficult short of experience to assess how one would react. . . . [Most] couples were apprehensive that they would react with jealousy and find the involvement disruptive. Rather than finding these fears justified most couples described their experience as one of release (no pun intended). The main components in this release were probably relief of simple acceptability and performance anxieties. (1974, 159–68)

Comfort goes on to state that most participating couples at Sandstone went to explore how such an experience would affect them as a couple. Nick reported that his group sex experiences with Rita left him feeling "a little naughty and adventurous." These experiences also renewed his emotional interest in Rita, which dissipated only when the issue of children and long-term family commitments emerged.

The third and final stage of Fierstein's developmental process is that of a couple's emergence into a larger social network involving children, or at least an extended family. In this phase, we again see many of Levinson's life structure components coalescing. For Nick Orren this phase clearly begins with his relationship to Dana. Not only has he completed his graduate work and secured a professorship, but he marries, has children, and moves into an extended social network. It could be argued that Dana represents Nick's resolution of many of the dichotomies evidenced earlier in his life. He did not want to be in the land development business, nor did he want to stay involved with a free clinic as he had when he was with Rita. Teaching represents his resolution of these divergent professional options, while Dana represents a personal resolution of the various social options he had explored. The evolution of Nick's case demonstrates how the various life structure components are constantly interacting and how our intimate involvements are frequently an integral part of our overall development.

To some people the varied sexual and social experiences of Nick might seem extreme or even promiscuous. I would argue that there are no universal standards for evaluating anyone's sexual development, nor should there be, except in situations involving exploitation or abuse. From Nick's perspective, his own sexual evolution was a long and complex process that he evaluated as productive. Using Levinson's concept of a life structure and Fierstein's sexual developmental phases, we can see Nick's case as a search to resolve several personal dichotomies while integrating his life structure components. Though Nick engaged in some activities that are not socially sanctioned, he never embraced a truly stigmatized sexual life-style.

Our next case study reviews the life of Tori Montgomery. Her sexual life is not as varied as Nick's but has an added twist—since she is a lesbian. Tori had to learn about living a stigmatized sexual life-style.

References and Suggested Readings

Comfort, Alex, ed. *More Joy of Sex.* New York: Simon and Schuster, 1974.

Fierstein, Harvey. *Safe Sex.* New York: Macmillan, 1988.

———. *Torch Song Trilogy.* New York: Gay Presses of New York, 1978.

Laing, R.D. *Knots.* New York: Vintage Books, 1970.

Levinson, Daniel, Charlotte Darrow, Edward Klein, Maria Levinson, and Braxton McKee. *The Seasons of a Man's Life.* New York: Ballantine Books, 1978.

Olds, Sally. *The Eternal Garden: Seasons of Our Sexuality.* New York: Time Books, 1985.

DISCUSSION AREAS

1. Nick's early sexual experience, that of the children performing a strip-tease show, is not unlike many early sexual experiences. The much-discussed "playing doctor" is a common experience among young children. What were your first sexual experiences? Do you think these had any influence on your later sexual development? How did your family react to such experiences, if they knew about them?

2. Nick discussed an early sex education class he had in the sixth grade. He described a filmstrip portraying Johnny Sperm and Susie Egg. There is much debate today about the role and function of sex education. What sort of formal sex education did you receive in school? Do you think you received enough sex education? Is there a danger of sex education being too explicit or introduced at too early an age? If you have children, or are planning to have children, what would you want their formal sex education to be like? What informal education would you provide?

3. Nick also related an early masturbation experience with his cousin, Carl. Traditionally, some psychiatrists have treated these experiences as evidence of latent homosexuality. For Nick, such experiences seemed to have little impact. Kinsey and associates have reported that many young people have some form of early homosexual experience. Have you had such experiences? Did they seem significant or important to you?

4. Nick discussed dating Anna in high school, primarily for social reasons. During the interview, he even reflected on the fact that he probably did not even like her as a person. How often do you think a person's social position influences who they date? How do you think a partner's social position has influenced or could influence your relationships?

5. Nick's older friend Ents served as a preliminary role model for Nick's sexual development. Research has shown that more information about sexuality is passed on from peers rather than schools or parents. Do you think such a role model is useful? Have you had such a role model? Ideally, what should a role model teach us? How did you react to Nick's watching Ents and his girlfriend having sex? More recently, some home video enthusiasts are filming themselves during sex. How do you feel about such activities?

6. While Nick cared about Kristin, during their separation he became involved with Laura. Many people report that separation can be traumatic, even destructive, to an intimate relationship. Do you think this is usually the case? If you were involved in a relationship you wanted to preserve, how might you deal with a long separation?

7. Laura came from a wealthy family, in which she was always encouraged to develop her own sexuality. How do you think wealth affects sexual behavior and attitudes?

8. Free-clinic colleague Rita certainly represented a new type of lover for Nick. Many writers have noted that we often engage in a rebound effect: when one relationship ends, we often begin another one that is in sharp contrast to the one that just ended. Do you think Nick's relationship with Rita was primarily caused by this rebound effect? Nick's relationship with Rita also had novel dimensions, including drugs, group sex, and a generally more experimental sexual life-style. What do you think of these experiences?

9. Nick decided to abort the baby he had conceived with Rita. Given the circumstances as outlined in the case, do you think this was the best thing to do? Why or why not? Should Nick have been the one to initiate this decision? The abortion issue is currently extremely controversial. What are your feelings on the subject? If you are prochoice, do you feel you adequately understand the right-to-life position? Or, if you are a right-to-life supporter, do you think you fully understand the prochoice position? How would you handle an unplanned pregnancy?

10. Nick's relationship with Marie represented a relatively stable period in his sexual development. Do you think we choose a relationship that ultimately satisfies only our needs at that time? This idea is certainly in contrast to the romantic notion that love, itself, determines a relationship. On a functional level, Marie appeared to be exactly what Nick needed while pursuing his graduate work. Do you think most of us pick relationships and stay in relationships that satisfy our basic needs? Why do some people stay in relationships that seem to satisfy so few of their basic needs?

11. Nick described Dana as the enduring answer to a long quest. Do you believe that? Do you think it is necessary to have a number of sexual relationships in order to find out who you are? Do you think a person can have too many sexual relationships? What do you see as the most significant influence in your own sexual development? What do you think contributes to a high-quality relationship? Are some qualities essential?

12. Nick described his relationship with Dana as going through "peaks and valleys." In our culture the myth of romance is that it is supposed to conquer many, if not all, adversities. In long-term relationships, how have you dealt with the "peaks and valleys"? Do you think it is possible or even reasonable to assume that two people in love can "live happily ever after"?

4
Growing up as a Lesbian:
Case Study of Tori Montgomery

Tori Montgomery has the attentive eyes of someone who does not miss much. Her presentation of self seems direct and honest. Though she does not dress to make a fashion statement, her natural femininity shines through. Though only thirty years old, she exudes a confident sense of purpose and direction normally found among older adults. One suspects she would be quite lively at the right party.

Tori's parents and two older brothers lived in Chicago's prosperous North Shore area and enjoyed an upper-class life-style. Tori's mother and father were close to each other but aloof with their children. The family was Episcopalian and fairly religious, although Tori said they were liberals politically and philosophically. The children were all sent to private religious schools and encouraged to socialize in various religious organizations. Tori had a typical early childhood and remembers nothing particularly distinctive about it. The family enjoyed a pleasant and materially comfortable life.

In kindergarten she had a crush on her female teacher, who talked to Tori more than her parents did. Tori's interest was based on simple admiration and the attention she received from this teacher.

Even though Tori had a small number of close friends in elementary school, she still felt herself to be something of an outcast. She reported feeling overly shy, and in many regards she was never part of the accepted "in" crowd. Tori's shyness and social isolation escalated as she entered junior high.

Also in junior high school, Tori began to realize that the other girls her age were far more interested in boys than she was. This was not at first a major issue, but it became increasingly significant as time passed.

At age fourteen Tori realized she was gay.

I was at home by myself. Everyone else had left. We had cable television, and I was watching TV. The movie *The Hunger* came on with David Bowie. In the movie there were two women having sex with each other and [clicks fingers] whamo! That is when I realized I was gay. That was the instant where I finally realized that was it. It was not like I had never had these feelings before, it was just at that moment that I knew what they meant. It scared me a lot. It really frightened me. It frightened me to put that label on myself—the label of lesbian. I said *lesbian* out loud and oh wow, was I frightened! It did not hurt but it was a shock. And of course I had heard about it being pretty bad—I mean I was brought up that way. And I knew that society did not like it, and it was quite a shock to know I would have to live with that label for the rest of my life.

Being gay and being attracted to other women were not the major causes of Tori's emerging apprehensions. She consistently reported that what alarmed her the most was society's connotations for the term *lesbian*. Even at fourteen Tori realized that this was not a socially accepted sexual life-style. Realizing she had clear and distinct sexual feelings about other women, Tori began to wrestle with how these feelings would affect her life.

For a year after her realization, Tori did not confide her feelings to anyone. Eventually, however, she decided to tell her junior high basketball coach.

The first person I ever told was my basketball coach. It was hard. I could not even say it. I just wrote it on a slip of paper: "I think I am gay." I handed it to her and started crying. She handled it well. She talked to me about it, and she did not treat it like it was any big deal. She was not gay, but she had been around it. She said, "Just go ahead and grow up, and if you are still gay, then you are gay." She told me it would be okay. I think the main thing was having someone to tell. And every time I have told someone since, it does get a little bit easier. Of course, it is not easy when they react in a condemning way, because that is real hard, but overall it does get easier. I think you just become more accepting of yourself as you tell other people and as you live with it.

As Tori entered high school, her concerns about being shy and not being part of the social mainstream increased. She also wanted to have a friend in whom she could confide about being gay. That summer Tori told a companion at a summer Young Life (Christian) camp that she was gay. The girl believed this was a major religious problem and told Mike, the camp counselor. Mike immediately confronted Tori in a most vitriolic manner.

Mike, the Bible Basher, said to me, "You are going to go to hell. This [gayness] is not part of God's plan. You are going to rot in hell." I think Mike is an asshole. While I am not religious anymore, I do believe in God. I just do not believe I am going to go to hell for being gay.

Tori's confrontation with Mike ended her high school commitment to established religion. As Tori moved away from her religious associations and her circle of religious peers, she again found her feelings of loneliness and separateness increasing.

During high school Tori met no lesbians her own age. The one opportunity to meet another lesbian in high school was set up by one of Tori's classmates. This friend knew an older lesbian woman, Jill, who attended a nearby college. Over dinner Jill tried to reassure Tori that her feelings about being gay were all right.

Tori did not feel comfortable with Jill, although she did contact her later that year when she realized she was falling in love with a student in her high school. Tori wanted Jill's advice about approaching this woman and revealing her romantic feelings. Jill encouraged Tori to express her romantic feelings, but she also warned her that the other woman would probably not reciprocate. Following Jill's advice, Tori talked to the woman, who turned out to be very religious and straight and who told Tori she would pray for her soul.

As she graduated from high school, Tori decided it would be best for her and her family if she attended a distant college. She picked a medium-sized state university in the western United States simply because her family had passed through that town on a family vacation. Arriving there, she realized that she did not know a single person in town. Her first year of college was the most difficult period in her life, with the loneliness and isolation that had haunted her ever since grade school contributing to her poor self-image. During these extreme periods of loneliness and low self-esteem, Tori thought about suicide.

What Tori missed most during her first year of college was a good friend. She had not yet learned how important a friend/lover could be, and she had not yet experienced the fulfillment possible in a sexually intimate relationship.

The person at college she admired the most was the female resident assistant in her dorm. In a series of letters to her R.A., Tori began to describe her feelings of loneliness and severe depression. The letters, while not blatantly romantic, subtly revealed her romantic feelings toward this woman. The R.A. showed them to the head resident because she believed Tori might be suicidal. The head resident talked to Tori, explaining that she herself was gay and that she could certainly understand and empathize with Tori's estrangement. Tori reported that she found this concern and empathy most welcome, and she began socializing with the head resident, Gail, at various campus events. Within a couple of weeks, the relationship turned personal and eventually sexual.

Tori's relationship with Gail lasted almost a year and proved to be a major turning point in her life. Gail was ten years older than Tori and had good contacts within the local lesbian community. She cared deeply about Tori and in many ways proved to be not only Tori's first lover but an excellent mentor as well. While Tori felt, in hindsight, that she was too dependent in the relationship, she did learn a great deal from Gail. Overall, the relationship did wonderful things for Tori's self-esteem. They spent lots of time together, and Tori found that their relationship made her life intrinsically rewarding.

> We spent a lot of time together. It was great. We spent Thanksgiving and some of Christmas break together, and that too was great. It was wonderful to have someone to love and to spend all of those times together. We shared a great deal, and I grew a lot through this relationship. We were the best of friends, and I loved our erotic, sensual lovemaking. The awakening of my sexual self certainly helped my self-esteem.

In addition to her improved self-esteem and emotional growth, Tori became less sensitive to public opinion and more accepting of her own body and sexuality. Since she had had strong sexual feelings about other women for a number of years, it was gratifying finally to learn how to express those feelings and share them with Gail. Although she enjoyed having sex with Gail, she felt that overall their friendship was more important than their sexual relationship.

Tori's relationship with Gail began to falter about eight or nine months after they became involved. Gail's supervisor at the university expressed concern about some stories circulating in the dorm regarding Gail's relationship with Tori. Ironically, just as Gail became increasingly agitated about these negative questions from her boss, she also started showing increasing affection toward Tori. Tori became alarmed by this new inconsistency; she was committed to their relationship, but she did not feel secure enough to demand any kind of resolution to these emerging inconsistencies. Finally, Gail told Tori that she felt it would be better if they did not see each other for a while. This crushed Tori.

After her relationship with Gail ended, Tori reappraised her situation. In retrospect, she believed she had been overly dependent on Gail and that their age difference made it difficult for them to plan a common future together. Gail had already had several significant relationships while Tori had just begun to develop her sexual identity. Tori began to wonder how she would grow and change within other relationships.

A year after separating from Gail, Tori went to a national conference of lesbians, gays, and bisexuals. The conference, held in San Francisco, proved interesting. The Ku Klux Klan picketed the meeting, and during the excitement Tori had what she described as a "minifling." After Tori met another lesbian at the conference whom she found socially and sexually attractive, they went for a walk and kissed. Since Tori took the initiative in this encounter, she developed new confidence in herself and her lesbianism. Her earlier problem of low self-esteem was vanishing.

For several months after the conference, Tori continued to be socially active within the lesbian community. On the door of her dormitory room, she displayed several pink flamingos, a national symbol of lesbians, and on her truck she placed a pink triangle, as a sign of solidarity within the local lesbian community.

Eventually, at a function hosted by the local lesbian bookstore, Tori met Joan, who also attended the university. Sharing several common interests, Tori and Joan quickly became good friends. In an interesting reversal of roles, Joan lacked self-confidence and Tori found herself encouraging Joan to be more self-assured. Later they became lovers, with the sexual dimension of their relationship solidifying an already solid friendship. Their relationship lasted for the next two years, during which time they both matured individually and as a couple. One of the major issues Tori resolved during this time was telling her parents that she was gay. She had always wanted to share her sexual orientation with her parents but was always afraid they would condemn and ostracize her. However, during her relationship with Joan, she felt it was important to begin creating a life that she could share with her family, and in this way, she realized it was time to let them know she was gay. To do this, Tori bought a book entitled *Beyond Acceptance: Parents of Lesbians and Gays Talk about Their Experiences* (Wirth and Wirth 1986). She took this book home on a visit to her parents with the intention of telling them directly about her being gay and giving them the book. Upon arriving home, she decided to confront this issue indirectly by leaving the book in a place where her parents would clearly see it. Shortly thereafter, her mother confronted her.

Mom said, "Your father and I have always wanted the best for you." Bingo, I knew it was coming. She got into this thing about finding the book and asking me if I was confused or had some questions. And then she said, "Probably I am just overreacting, right?" And I told her, "No! You are not overreacting." Then she said, "You cannot be serious—you just cannot be . . ." "Yes, Mom, I am gay . . ." So she started crying real hard, and I felt so bad. I felt awful. The look on her face, the tenor of her voice, and the way she was crying—it was heart-wrenching. I wanted to say, "Look, Mom, I was only kidding—I am not gay." But I could not lie.

Needless to say, the next few days at home were not particularly pleasant for anyone. Her father, who found out the following day, was especially angry. After he moved beyond disbelief, he became agitated. Tori returned to school concerned over whether she had done the right thing. But as time passed, her parents became more understanding. Tori felt time alone helped her parents to begin tolerating her lesbianism. Eventually, her father came to visit and in his own way tried to let her know that he would tolerate her homosexuality.

> My dad said, "What you want to do with your life is up to you—we cannot stop you. It does not matter to me how you want to get your orgasms." I was really pissed off. I felt that his attitude was totally degrading. I know he was trying to show some tolerance for my life-style, but he said it in such a base, crass way. I still do not think he has a good understanding of my relationships or feelings. Maybe he never will.

While her parents are tolerating her sexual life-style, Tori remains convinced that they are obsessed with their image in the community. Her parents feel that if their friends and neighbors learned that Tori is gay it would be a major scandal, and they want Tori to keep her sexual life-style secret. Tori is not particularly pleased about this, nor does she believe the projected scandal would actually materialize, even if her parents' friends did find out.

Shortly after Tori's reconciliation meeting with her father, Tori's relationship with Joan began to deteriorate. There were no unpleasant or harsh scenes; the two of them just began to drift apart. Becoming less and less interested in spending time together, they finally separated as friends. Tori continues, on occasion, to socialize with Joan, but their romance has definitely evaporated.

This second relationship was valuable to Tori in new ways. With added maturity and a constantly improving self-image, Tori felt her relationship with Joan was definitely one in which the two of them played a more equal role. Though she had learned much in her relationship with Gail, her relationship with Joan was much more powerful, because of this equality.

Tori remains politically and socially active within the lesbian community, and she no longer feels like an outsider. Currently celibate, she believes she will have a significant and long-lasting relationship, but at this point she seems content to wait until the right situation emerges.

Being active in the gay community and having several gay male friends, Tori is alarmed about AIDS.

> Even though I am not in a high-risk bracket, it scares me. Even though you cannot contract AIDS through kissing or other casual

stuff, it is still in the back of my mind. I think now I would not get into a deep relationship with someone unless I knew a lot about her background and she was willing to get tested with me. Even though I have only had two relationships, my friends and I did get tested just to know if we had it. We just wanted to know to be real sure. Now I have been tested and I can tell a prospective partner that I did test negative.

Reflecting on sex in general, Tori had this to say:

I do not believe in sex for sex's sake. I believe in making love. I just do not think that casual sex would mean that much to me. I do not think of my relationships with women as being dramatically different from many of those found in the heterosexual world. I am not sure I understand why our society places so much emphasis on the sexes of lovers. I am committed to basic feminist principles, but I do not believe that I hate men or feel in any way the need to separate our society by sex. I think, in many ways, my life is just like anybody else's life, with the statistical exception that I love people of the same sex.

Tori feels her initial anxieties and apprehensions about being a lesbian have generally been successfully resolved. She offered the following piece of advice to other young women who feel they might be lesbians:

Do not be ashamed of being gay. Do not be ashamed of who you are. And if those around you tell you not to be gay, my advice is to follow your heart. If you are in love with a woman, be in love with that woman. And if you fall in love with a man, love that man. Just do not let society put you down or get you down. And if people put you down for what you really feel, then you are going to have to learn to deal with their put-downs and to rely on yourself and grow stronger from society's ostracism. You have to keep going and doing what your heart tells you to. If you are afraid, with nobody to talk to, try and find a [lesbian] community. One out of ten are gay. There have to be others around. Almost all big metropolitan areas have gay communities. The point is, you are not alone and there are others like you who are willing to help. In time, you will probably come to value your lesbianism and the personal growth that comes with it.

ANALYSIS

The Social Construction of Sexuality

Tori Montgomery wrestled with what it means to be a woman, a feminist, and a lesbian. Although these issues do not have to be related, there are some engaging connections, even beyond Tori's case.

In their book *Powers of Desire: The Politics of Sexuality* (1984), Ann Snitow, Christine Stansell, and Sharon Thompson contend that sexuality in modern American culture faces some interesting contradictions:

> In spite of its publicity, sex remains oddly taboo, particularly for women. The widespread exposure to sexual imagery and talk seems not to have made a dent in the embarrassment. The sexual shame that begins in childhood—and which the entire culture endlessly recreates—keeps the sense of taboo alive even in a blitz of the sexually explicit. (1984, 9)

Snitow, Stansell, and Thompson (1984) make the argument that sexuality as a conscious human experience is constructed. There is a dazzling array of possibilities inherent in this idea. Indeed, if the biological and social dimensions of sexuality are only antecedents rather than outright determinants of human sexuality, then the range of our sexuality is only limited by our concepts and ideas about it. This does not mean we can ignore the physiological components of sexual activity, but it does suggest that the meanings of sexuality are neither predetermined nor fixed. Our ideas about sexuality become its constructs. And clearly our ideas about sexuality and its attendant social matrix are changing.

> There is no escaping it: sex as refuge, or sex as sacrament, or sex as wild, natural, dark, and instinctual expression—all these are ideas about sex, and ideas about sex have never been more obvious than now, when sex is no longer coterminous with the family, or with procreation, or with sin. Indeed, historical changes that often seem to be trivializing sex are, at the same time, making of it a separate and newly meaningful category of experience.
>
> In recent decades, Americans have experienced major shifts in what the culture expects from men, women, and sex. Transformations in work, family, gender—often in the course of one lifetime—foster rapidly changing sexual experiences. Marriage, childbearing, and childrearing are increasingly brief experiences for most Americans. The fertility rate has reached its lowest point in U.S. history. The stereotype of the nuclear family—man at work, woman at home caring full time for two or more children—is a reality for fewer and fewer people (14 percent at this writing). The average marriage lasts five years, one of every three ends in divorce. Three-quarters of all married women have jobs; a single woman heads one in every seven households; lesbians are struggling for, and in

many cases winning, custody of their children; and lesbian and gay cultures are sketching the bases for new social structures. (Snitow, Stansell, and Thompson 1984, 11)

The fact that gay/lesbian relationships have no rigidly defined gender role models that must be followed gives many gays the flexibility to determine sexual roles for themselves. In this sense, Tori's relationships with both Joan and Gail had a potential role flexibility not found in many heterosexual relationships.

The Future of Sexual Constructs

Snitow, Stansell, and Thompson pursue this concept of the social construction of sexuality further by asking what social forces and ideas will shape the ever-changing dimensions of contemporary sexuality for heterosexuals as well as gays. As feminists they see this molding of sexuality to be primarily a political process. They raise some intriguing questions as to what forms sexuality should take and indeed what the future of sexuality might hold.

We want sexual information and opportunities for the young, the old, the handicapped, and all groups for whom sex has been taboo. We want civil rights for all sexual minorities. But what else? What aspects of sex can and should be publicly debated? What should political activism about sex look like? What erotic experiences will we encourage in our children? Do we favor the constraint of some kinds of sexual expression? Do we have any concept of a sexual "public good"? Or, if we advocate a more libertarian position (anything goes, as long as all parties consent), what are the limits of that consent? (1984, 12)

Lesbian versus Heterosexual Perspectives

Let us turn now to one of the earlier claims that gays are creating "bases for new social structures." Janice Raymond's book *A Passion for Friends: Towards a Philosophy of Female Affection* (1986) talks about moving beyond "hetero-reality" (or the reality emerging out of contemporary heterosexuality) to a world of "gyn/affection" a reality emergent from female relationships. Raymond notes how female friendships (and love relationships) often have qualities of compassion and mutual respect not found in "hetero-reality." Yet such relationships are often discounted or trivialized by society. Indeed, she disputes the common assumption that women without men are women without either company or companionship. Raymond talks about how empowering woman-to-woman relationships should benefit all of us. By envisioning a plurality of social possibilities we will have options beyond the often stridently competitive macho-world of hetero-reality. Accrediting a wider range of woman-to-woman affections should also accredit a wider range of man-to-man affections without triggering the traditional homophobic assumptions about latent homosexuality.

In Tori Montgomery's life, her friendship with Gail (which ultimately became sexual) embodied many of the positive dimensions of Raymond's gyn/affection. Her relationship with Gail improved her self-esteem, helped her mature emotionally, and made her more aware and accepting of her own sexuality. Also, Gail's familiarity with the local lesbian community helped Tori gain support and guidance, even after her relationship with Gail ended. This support helped Tori deal with some of the issues particular to lesbians.

Coming out of the Closet

While Tori's case is quite comparable to that of many young heterosexual women, in a few notable regards it is different. Tori's first gay issue was her almost instinctive awareness that being gay was not going to be an easy thing to share with other people. It took her almost a year before she mustered the courage to share this with her basketball coach. The coach's reaction was probably as supportive as one could hope, given society's current reservations about gay life-styles.

JoAnn Loulan defines this lesbian coming-out process thus:

> Coming out is a long process and many of us are engaged in it most of our lives. Recognizing our desire to be as fully with women as possible, acting on that desire, and acknowledging that truth to ourselves and others is the coming-out process. (1984, 117)

Another series of issues that Tori confronted because she was a lesbian involved learning how to accept her own sexual feelings and share those with other women. Don Clark has written a widely read book on this subject for both gay men and lesbians. In *The New Loving Someone Gay* (1987) he deals with issues ranging from how to accept and express one's homosexual feelings, to discussions of gay life-styles for families and friends of gays.

Tori also debated how to tell her parents she was gay. As was mentioned earlier, she used Marian and Arthur Wirth's book *Beyond Acceptance: Parents of Lesbians and Gays Talk about Their Experiences* (1986) to help her parents move beyond accepting her gayness to understanding and possibly even appreciating it. As evidenced by her father's remark,

"It does not matter to me how you get your orgasms," this process is not exactly finished.

Gay Issues

For Tori being a lesbian also created problems with some of her female friends. We all have friends with whom we do not want to be sexual. But because many of Tori's friends were not familiar with lesbian life-styles, they found it difficult to be her friend. They were hesitant to deal with an unfamiliar sexual orientation; indeed, it was safer to quit being her friend. Tori also continues searching for a church to support her both as a human being and as a lesbian.

Tori continues to want a long-term relationship with a lover. Therapist Betty Berzon in her book *Permanent Partners: Building Gay and Lesbian Relationships That Last* (1988) analyzes the special problems inherent in gay and lesbian long-term relationships. According to Berzon, one serious problem in maintaining a long-term gay relationship is society's lack of structural supports (like the institution of marriage, with its recognition and privileges). For the interested student Berzon discusses a wide range of potential problems in long-term gay relationships and various creative solutions.

By looking at the case study of Tori Montgomery, we begin to understand what a powerful influence society has in shaping both our individual and collective constructions of sexuality. Social attitudes toward lesbian life-styles are often quite negative or at least intolerant. For people like Tori these attitudes seem to complicate their lives unnecessarily, forcing their own personal issues of sexual exploration and development to occur within this critical environment. This has to compound an already complicated process.

In our next case study we will look at the life of Patrick Graddy, a Catholic priest. Father Graddy has a sexual life-style, which, like Tori's, society has prejudged.

References and Suggested Readings

Berzon, Betty. *Permanent Partners: Building Gay and Lesbian Relationships That Last*. New York: Dutton, 1988.

Clark, Don. *The New Loving Someone Gay*. New York: Celestial Arts, 1987.

Loulan, JoAnn. *Lesbian Sex*. San Francisco: Spinsters/Aunt Lute Press, 1984.

Raymond, Janice. *A Passion for Friends: Towards a Philosophy of Female Affection*. Boston: Beacon Press, 1986.

Snitow, Ann, Christine Stansell, and Sharon Thompson. *Powers of Desire: The Politics of Sexuality*. New York: New Feminist Library, 1984.

Wirth, Marian, and Arthur Wirth. *Beyond Acceptance: Parents of Lesbians and Gays Talk about Their Experiences*. Englewood Cliffs, N.J.: Prentice Hall, 1986.

DISCUSSION AREAS

1. Tori reported that by age fourteen she realized she was a lesbian. What sort of sexual awareness did you have by that age? How did you handle your emerging sexuality? Many gays report that growing up as a homosexual is complicated because there are no visible role models for young gay people. Do you agree? Do you think Tori would have benefited from more gay social support as a junior high or high school student? Do you think high schools should have gay support groups?

2. Though Tori had some initial excitement about her sexual feelings, she also became anguished when she realized that the term *lesbian* would be applied to her. How do you think labels affect our sexual lives and our images of ourselves? Do you think society has been fair in its labeling of homosexual life-styles?

3. About a year after Tori realized she was a lesbian, she told her basketball coach. Do you think her basketball coach reacted appropriately? What would be your reaction? Could her basketball coach have done more? What are the responsibilities of teachers in junior high and high school to help their students with sexual issues? Should such issues just be left to the parents or religious institutions? Who helped you with your sexual development?

4. Tori's religious friends, and in particular Mike, responded very negatively to Tori's gayness. Would your church support or encourage this kind of behavior? Do you think churches should be more understanding of homosexuality?

5. Do you think feelings of extreme loneliness are that unusual among young people today? While Tori felt that her initial loneliness at college had nothing to do with being a lesbian, it is obvious that her first relationship helped many of her insecurities dissipate. Do you think Tori's feelings of loneliness were compounded by her being gay? How have your sexual relationships influenced your identity and overall sense of confidence?

6. Tori's first intimate relationship with Gail proved pivotal in her life. How did your first relationship influence you? Do you think Tori's relationship differed emotionally in any significant way from the kind of relationships many heterosexuals have?

7. Tori's relationship with Joan was stronger because of her involvement with Gail. In this sense, what she had learned from her first relationship carried over into her second involvement. How have your earlier relationships influenced your later relationships?

8. Tori had a great deal of difficulty telling her parents she was gay. How would your parents react to such information? Do you think

Tori did the right thing by telling them? Do you think her parents' friends really would be traumatized if they found out she was gay? Do you think Tori handled this part of her "coming out" well?

9. Tori's association with the gay community has led her into direct contact with many people who are dealing with AIDS. Though Tori is not in a high vulnerability bracket, she definitely has concerns about AIDS. Has AIDS affected your sexual life? What are your concerns about AIDS?

10. Near the end of the interview, Tori stated that her relationships were not significantly different from heterosexual relationships except that society does not approve of gay life-styles. Do you agree? Do you think society is overly concerned about the sex of partners in a sexual relationship?

11. Tori's last statement of support for other students who might be gay raises some interesting issues. What was your reaction to that statement? Do you think a statement like Tori's should be widely distributed to junior high or high school students? Why do you think some people are so antagonistic to lesbians? Do you think people are even more antagonistic to gay men?

12. While sensitive to the destructive potential of labels, Tori mentioned how glad she was not to be a foo-foo. A foo-foo, in gay parlance, is a woman who, being rather foolish, makes an excessive effort to impress men. (*Foo-foo* has also been used as a derogatory term for an extraeffeminate gay male.) Do you think heterosexual women in general waste too much time and effort trying to impress men? Do you think our advertising industry exploits our insecurities and desire to impress the opposite sex? Do you think some men spend too much time trying to impress women?

5

Living a Life of Committed Celibacy within a Sexual Society: Case Study of Father Patrick Graddy

Father Patrick Graddy, a well-built man in his late forties, has a disarming boy-next-door smile that immediately makes him charming. While he clearly has the seriousness of his spiritual convictions, his natural informality and friendliness shine through. His quick wit and dry sense of humor help make him a thoughtful and engaging conversationalist. Patrick's contemplative life-style has allowed him to ponder his own sexuality with a thoroughness rare in today's complicated and hectic world.

Born in Queens, New York, Patrick was a child during World War II. Patrick's parents married young: his mother was nineteen when she married and his father was twenty-two. The first of five children, Patrick has two brothers and two sisters. The children were born several years apart, and Patrick is sixteen years older than his youngest sibling.

Patrick reported being close to his mother, a kind and compassionate person who had primary responsibility for raising Patrick, his brothers, and sisters. Patrick's father had only a ninth-grade education and "lived in a small world." Patrick's father drank, occasionally excessively. This seemed to worsen his temper, which could be quite nasty at times. Patrick remembered his father on leave from the war visiting the family where Patrick, his mother, his brother, and an elderly aunt and uncle lived.

> I would say, even as a young kid, I was conscious of a distance between myself and my dad. I was afraid of my dad because of his bad temper. We were not close. My father was good around small children, but since he was at the war [World War II] when I was young, we never shared that closeness. My earliest recollection of Dad was one of him being mad at me and getting ready to bounce me off a wall, and my uncle grabbed him and made him put me down. I was about four when this happened.

With only a very limited education, Patrick's father was never able to secure a well-paying job. Although the family had the basic necessities of food, clothing, and shelter, their life was never materially comfortable, and this, combined with the father's bad temper and drinking problem, made Patrick's life at home difficult. Even as a small child, Patrick was aware of the limitations of his working-class family, and he describes his earliest experiences at school as being those of a young boy anxiously trying to win the respect of his peers and teachers.

> My temperament in grade school was always to be the best little boy in the world, a good student, very helpful, basically a nurturing kind of person, even back then. I was never good at sports— just a tremendous reader, good writer, interested in all kinds of stories, and generally interested in doing things that were perceived as helpful.

Despite his helpful attitude, Patrick saw himself as being somewhat unacceptable to his peers, his teachers, and perhaps even, to a certain extent, his family. He spent a lot of his youth trying to earn people's respect and admiration. At one point during the interview he said, "It is hard to believe that anybody would really love me, that is, if they really got to know me as the person I was." He felt unworthy of the attention and love that he did receive as a child.

When he was six, Patrick had his first sexual experience.

> I remember Mary Wells who lived down the street from us. Mary was the one whose mission in life was to make every boy on the block know how little girls were put together, and I remember standing in line on a vacant lot waiting with the other neighborhood boys to be introduced to the mysteries of female anatomy. Just as it was almost my turn, this neighbor came roaring out of his house yelling, "You kids get out of here! I know what you are doing!" And we all scattered to the four winds. It was quite an adventure, and I do not think my curiosity was satisfied.

Patrick recalled that when he was a young boy his family did not attend church regularly even though both his parents had been raised as Catholics.

> My family was nonpracticing Catholic, at least for a long time. All of the kids were baptized as Catholics, and all of us made our first communion. But there was a long period of time when we did not go to church on Sunday. From the time I was in the fourth grade until I was a sophomore in high school, we rarely went to church.

Patrick's time in grade school seemed uneventful except for the fact that he did exceptionally well in school. He had an average number of friends of both sexes and had the usual competitive relationship with the older of his two brothers and a good relationship with the older of his two sisters. Growing up, he hardly knew his youngest sister and youngest brother because they were so much younger than he.

Throughout grade school and until junior high, Patrick reported that sex and sexual issues were almost ignored in his life. However, during junior high Patrick found out more about sex and masturbation.

All through grade school right up until about seventh grade, there was not much of an emphasis on sexual matters. In our culture, in our family, in the town we lived in, and the age in which I lived, children could grow up without dealing much with sexual issues. I do remember, in junior high school we all started finding out about "It." And then there was the whispered talk and jokes. And I found out about masturbation from some of the other guys. I was not clever enough to figure that out for myself. When I started masturbating, I had no guilt because I did not realize that was part of my religious tradition. That [guilt] came later. When I was older and knew what that meant as a Catholic, I started bringing it [masturbation] under control. It was a typical adolescent struggle for a Catholic, and of course back then it was considered real wrong. Now it is considered wrong, but one does not torture oneself over it. Most people grow out of that [interest in masturbation].

Early in junior high, Patrick also decided to become a teacher. He enjoyed biology and science in general, and he did well in school. Since he was a good student who loved to read, the thought of sharing the academic life with students was intriguing. At this time he became close friends with a male biology teacher whom he admired a great deal. This teacher was bright and exceptionally good with students; he enjoyed teaching and was married, with several children. Patrick initially assumed this was the type of life-style he would develop.

During his sophomore year of high school, Patrick made several major decisions that ultimately changed his life. Though no one in his extended family had ever gone to college, he began taking college prep classes and doing well in them. Socializing with many of the brightest students in school and talking with these friends, he began considering humanity's purpose in life.

I remember when I was a sophomore in high school, I decided to start going to church. It was also about that time that I decided

I would like to try and become a priest. So for me, my decision to start going back to church and confession, mass, and communion were very much tied to my interest in the priesthood. I think this decision was based on several factors. I went to a good public school and I was in the college prep program. I had a lot of smart friends, but none of them had any strong religious beliefs. And during lunchtime they would often get into matters of philosophy and religion. Since I was one of the few Catholics around, even though I was a nonpracticing Catholic, I would be asked to explain or justify what we believed as Catholics. I started doing some reading, a couple of religious books plus the New Testament, to answer some of their questions. And it was out of my readings that I began to learn about my own religious tradition and began to personally be involved in that tradition. I would read in the New Testament where Jesus would say to Peter or James or John, "I want you to let go of your nets, park your boats, and come follow me. I will make you fishers of men." I really felt within my heart the invitation of the Lord to follow Him and be a priest.

With his awakening interest in Catholicism and his emerging desire to become a priest, Patrick found his attitudes about sexuality and women shifting. He no longer assumed that he would be a teacher with a family. He began to investigate the life of the clergy, and his attitudes toward subjects like masturbation, and sex in general, began to evolve, aligning more with established Catholic perspectives.

In reflecting about sex in high school, Father Graddy had this to say:

Sex for me in high school was really more an issue of relationships and romance rather than sex. I never really put pressure on myself to just do that [have sex].

By his junior year in high school, Patrick had established a strong interest in philosophy and religious theology, and in pursuing his dream to become a Catholic priest. To be more financially independent while pursuing these goals, he took a part-time job at a pet shop. Shortly before high school graduation Patrick met Shelly.

In high school I was just not quick with sports. I was skinny and a little shy. I remember, if there was a dance, it took me weeks to get up enough courage to ask a girl out. I never felt terribly self-confident. I did have a couple of girls as friends and a couple of girls that I really liked a lot but I did not have what I would call a hard-core girlfriend till I was a senior in high school. When

I was a senior, I met Shelly at a dance. She was from another high school. She came up to me to ask about a science fair project which I had completed. She had some pet mice, and she would come to the pet shop to get a little bag of food for them. Eventually she asked me out. We had a good time and after that started going out regularly. I felt very comfortable with her. I did not have to worry about what I was going to say or do around her. Shelly was attractive, smart, and comfortable with herself.

And then I got my letter of acceptance to Cathedral College in Brooklyn (preseminary) and part of that involved no dating, no socializing with women, period. It was a very black-and-white issue back then. So I went to see Shelly and told her I could never see her again. As I look back on that now, I wish I had handled that differently. I wish I had said to her that we should at least continue to be friends. I was reaching a point in my life where I was blossoming a bit in terms of my relationships with people and women my own age, and I think I could have bent the rules and continued seeing her at least as a friend. What I did was bring down a wall between myself and a little more than half the population of the world [women]. It took me many years before I overcame that wall.

After high school, Patrick began attending Cathedral College in Brooklyn to prepare for the seminary. He continued to live at home and, as he had throughout high school, continued working part-time in the pet shop. During this time he had virtually no contact with women except for members of his own family.

Later, during summer vacation from college, Patrick took a job at a camp for emotionally disturbed children on Long Island. Situated on five hundred lush acres, the camp was picturesque. Most of the staff were women counselors, and Patrick was one of only two men at the camp. During the first summer, he had a romantic friendship with a personable and attractive young woman. This summer was a special one for him because he cared deeply about the young woman, and, as with Shelly, he found it easy to be with her. The summer passed quickly, but upon his return to the seminary, the friendship dissolved. He frequently thought about this woman, even though nothing sexual had occurred between them.

After another academically successful year at Cathedral College, Patrick returned to the camp for a second summer. During that summer, Patrick met Monica, an exceptional individual who was bright, energetic, self-confident, and poised. She was also beautiful and came from a wealthy family. He described her as a "woman and a half." Patrick and Monica spent a lot of time with each other that summer, and she fell in love with him. However, Patrick kept his feelings for Monica in check for two reasons. First, because he was planning to become a priest, he felt it inappropriate to become sexual with Monica. Second, he also felt that Monica would probably never become serious and marry a person like him with limited prospects.

As the summer ended, Patrick lost contact with Monica. But he was later surprised to learn that Monica did marry a rather average-looking public school teacher who was really no more appealing than he. In reminiscing about his relationship with Monica, Patrick remains convinced that even had he known Monica might marry him, he probably would have chosen the priesthood anyway. Yet he continues to be amused about the possibility of what would have happened with Monica had he been a little more self-confident.

After these two romantic summers at camp, Patrick renewed his commitment to Catholicism and entered the seminary. At the seminary, Patrick reported that he became increasingly comfortable with his life of celibacy. He generally put the issue of his own sexuality aside.

> Being a priest meant that I would have to be celibate, and therefore I really did not have to think much more about my sexuality, of relating to women or about dealing with my feelings toward women. I put all that stuff up on a shelf. I do not think I was trying to hide from my sexuality, but I did have a sense of relief in that when I was accepted into the seminary I simply did not have to deal with my sexuality, and in some senses, with my intimate feelings. I felt I did not have to worry about those issues. Of course, later I came to realize that ignoring all these issues was simply not possible.

At twenty-six, Patrick Graddy was ordained as a priest in the Catholic Church. Having distinguished himself in the seminary, he had mastered much of the intellectual philosophy of the contemporary Catholic Church. Emotionally, however, Patrick still needed to mature.

> At twenty-six, when I was ordained, I was still a bit immature in my dealings with people. I was overly intellectual without enough coming from here [points to his heart]. My capacity for having a real deep and close relationship with anybody was very limited. I just had not learned how to do that yet.

After being ordained, Patrick had several parish assignments in which he dealt effectively with the intellectual needs of his parishioners. However, within the next four years he had three experiences that helped him remove the wall he had built to block out his emotional life and his feelings for women. First, Patrick and a fellow priest attended a marriage encounter weekend with fifteen married couples. This encounter weekend was designed to help couples explore their feelings and improve their communication skills. During this weekend Patrick became increasingly aware of many emotional issues within his own life which he had been ignoring. This was the beginning of his journey to become more aware of his own emotions.

Second, about this same time Patrick joined a fraternity for Catholic priests called Jesu Caritas (Latin for love of Jesus). In this fraternity, with five other priests who were all approximately the same age, Patrick began to share himself emotionally. For the next eighteen years, and continuing even now, this group of six priests meets once a month for a day of prayer and "a review of life." Patrick described this review as "a type of group spiritual discernment among close, intimate friends." After meeting and sharing for more than eighteen years, these priests have explored many personal, emotional, and spiritual issues together.

The third event that helped Patrick open up to the emotional issues in his life was his assignment to a Newman Center at a state university in southern California. During his second year at the Newman Center, Patrick met Tom.

> Probably the person who taught me the most about being in touch with myself and about love itself was Tom. One year after I came up to the university, Tom started there as a freshman. I have never met anybody in my life who is as loving a person [as Tom]. I have never allowed anyone to get as close to me as Tom. We love each other and we have shared so very much. You might call us soul-friends who share a powerful spiritual bond. What we really have is a sacramental friendship. I believe all God's grace is embodied and Tom is a great expression of God's love for me. And because of our friendship, I can now relate from here [gestures toward heart] as well as from here [gestures toward head]. Tom opened up my heart and taught me how to love myself just for being myself, and not because I had earned his love.

Patrick has a special relationship with Tom for a number of reasons. Though Tom is considerably younger than Patrick, in many ways Patrick felt they were equals. They shared a great deal with each other, including several vacations, but the most important thing that Patrick received from Tom was his unqualified love. Tom cared about, indeed loved, Patrick, not because he was a Catholic priest but because of the person that Patrick was and is. For Patrick, this friendship and love from Tom created a new integration between his intellectual and emotional life. For the first time ever, he told someone that he loved him.

Through all of these experiences Patrick found his Catholic teachings merging comfortably with his newfound emotional depth. Patrick now savors his friendships with both men and women and can be emotionally as well as intellectually accessible to his parishioners. Patrick is also aware of his own sexual feelings and had this to say about his current friendships and celibacy:

> Here I am as a person, leading the celibate life, and I am blessed with a number of loving and deep friendships that are spiritual, sexual, emotional. They are really all of these things except that there is no genital sex. For me celibate love includes warm, loving, and affectionate relationships with both men and women. However, there is always a tendency for that love to move towards a more complete and genital expression. And that is where the tension comes in. I find that at times I have gone too far in the physical expression of my love. I am always afraid of being selfish or of just using another person to satisfy my own deep emotional and sexual needs. As I am now allowing my relationships more depth, I suspect that this tension will increase. However, the alternative of bringing down that wall of separation between myself and other people is no longer acceptable. I will live with this tension as the price of developing a more loving heart.

Currently Father Graddy has a strong friendship with a widow named Lynn. If he ever made the decision to leave the priesthood, he believes he could have a satisfying marriage and sexual relationship with her. While we all ponder changes in our lives, Father Graddy has chosen to remain a member of the clergy and to share his intellectual and emotional life with his parish. Father Graddy seems to have found spiritual fulfillment as a celibate priest.

Patrick had these comments about the challenges of living a celibate life:

> I really think that one of the challenges of the celibate life is to open yourself up to all that you can learn from women. You need to be in touch with your own male and female dimensions. And I think a lot of men learn about that in marriage from their wives and thereby make that spiritual journey to become in touch with their feminine side. As a celibate, it requires a conscious effort to open yourself up.

Patrick's choice for a celibate life is just that—a choice. Since it is a conscious choice for him, he does not feel blindly trapped by his celibacy.

Celibacy is a form of love in which, instead of focusing your love on one person, you learn to focus on a whole community. And for a priest, that means learning to share his love with the whole community in which he lives. A priest must learn to love the community with the same power that a young man would try to bring to his bride or give to his family. That is the key to being fulfilled as a celibate. A priest's celibacy is not a closing of the heart or a pulling back, but rather one must learn to share one's love with a whole lot of people.

During the course of his interviews, Patrick talked a great deal about his own life and about how, from his perspective, sexuality can and should operate. He is concerned about how sex is often treated so casually that, in essence, it comes to mean very little (see Terry Grant's case, chapter 9). He emphasized that it is we who create the feelings attached to sex. For Patrick, if one is going to be sexually active, the key to having a meaningful sex life is to confine sex to marriage and the context of a committed relationship.

Patrick currently advises couples who are considering marriage, including his close friend Tom. He had the following sexual advice for such couples:

Lust is to sex what gluttony is to food. It is the misuse of a good thing. Without the sacramental bond of marriage and a committed relationship, sex does not reach its full human potential.

Christians believe that marriage is a sacrament. Somehow in the love between a man and a woman where there is that sacramental bond, you will find a human expression of love that is in the heart of God Himself.

ANALYSIS

Most of us do not consciously choose to be or not be sexually active. Our choices are usually more related to how we express our sexuality and with whom. Kinsey and associates (1948, 1953) have documented that for the vast majority of us genital sexuality is a natural part of our adult lives. For those who choose celibacy, the choice differs sharply from the overall cultural pattern of sexual expression. Celibates, as outsiders to this pattern, have a perspective on sexuality not readily available to the sexually involved.

Historical Celibacy

The term *celibacy* is derived from the Latin word *caelebs,* which is usually translated as meaning "single" or "alone." Celibacy means different things to different people, but it has been present throughout human history. Hinduism, one of the oldest religions, has four basic stages of spiritual development. The first and the fourth, *Bramacarya,* are stages in which the spiritual devotee remains celibate. Historically in Judaism, young men were expected to marry and be sexually active; however, many rabbis left their wives for years in order to study the Torah, for it was assumed that in separating from their wives they would be able to concentrate on the spiritual fulfillment that studying the Torah would bring. Among the various Christian churches, the Roman Catholic faith is most often associated with issues of celibacy, although it was not until the year 1123 that the first Lateran Council required universal celibacy for the entire Catholic clergy. Goergen reported in 1975 that some 1.5 million Roman Catholic men and women have taken vows to lead celibate lives.

So the question becomes, what does a renunciation of sexual contact with a partner or with oneself really mean? For the purposes of this analysis, we will focus almost exclusively on how it affects Catholic priests. We do this simply because little has been written about choosing celibacy for reasons other than those of religion. One notable exception is Swami Bhaktipada's new book *The Joy of No Sex: How to Stop Worrying About AIDS and Start Living Happily Without Sex.* In this book, Bhaktipada contends that living the life of celibacy is not only spiritually more fulfilling, but, because of the AIDS crisis, it is the most logical sexual life-style.

Celibacy in the Catholic Church

So what does a celibate commitment mean to those Catholic men and women who have chosen this life-style? Though there are many writers on the subject, their ideas about celibacy vary. The Reverend David Knight sees celibacy this way:

> By renunciation of marriage the celibate is making a very specific statement, which is a profession of faith: "I renounce marriage as a way of saying that I really believe that God is offering Himself to all believers as an object of spousal love on earth. I renounce marriage to show (and to realize within myself) that I believe I can have, through grace, a relationship of love on earth with Jesus Christ right now which is as real, as satisfying, and as developmental of me as a loving person, as the relationship of marriage would be with another concrete human being." Celibacy is a way of putting flesh behind one's words. (1985, 14–15)

Charles Gallagher and Thomas Vandenburg discuss celibacy in their book *Celibacy Myth: Loving for Life* as a charism. Charism, as they use the term, is a divinely inspired gift, and this way of renouncing sexual behavior becomes a gift offered up to God. Gallagher and Vandenburg have this to say about celibacy as charism:

> This is the point of the celibacy charism. It is not a renunciation; it is an affirmation. Celibacy is a charism of relationship. It has to do with the relationship of a priest with his people, his bonding with them. It is about his placing his happiness in their hands, his act of faith that they will make his life fulfilling by the love they pour out on him. Celibacy is what enables a priest to say to the faithful, "I trust you; I believe you; I make myself yours." (1987, 15)

But even beyond these conceptual definitions, the more interesting question remains, what does celibacy as a sexual life-style mean within the lives of the people who have chosen it? The research literature indicates that for many Roman Catholic priests and nuns, the life of celibacy is often not fully understood when it is initially chosen. Just like sexually active people, celibates often take many years to understand what their sexual choices will mean to them. At first, Patrick assumed that he should build a wall to block off his feelings, particularly toward women. However, he eventually came to a broader understanding of what celibacy could mean. Goergen talks about the need to seek this broader understanding of celibacy:

> Celibacy is an ideal, not the only Christian ideal but still an ideal. Ideals always have been and always will be attractive. In this sense celibacy is attractive, not only to mature people but to naive people as well. When one is first attracted to celibacy, he or she may not have a deep understanding of himself or herself or of that which draws him or her forward. Eventually he or she must seek this understanding. (1975, 109)

Just as we saw in Patrick's case, seeking this broader understanding of celibacy is not an easy process. Indeed, many who initially choose celibacy avoid sexual involvements by avoiding their own feelings. However, for many priests such emotional detachment becomes overly confining and lonely. An apparently common solution to this problem is to become familiar with one's emotional self, integrating both the masculine and feminine dimensions of one's own psyche.

Gallagher and Vandenburg talk about how they, like Patrick, became aware of these emotional issues during a marriage encounter group.

> It was just this type of priest who was often deeply moved by such experiences as Marriage Encounter. In a rather dramatic fashion, they encountered themselves and their *anima*, possibly for the first time. It was nothing short of a profound revelation. In witnessing the tenderness of the husbands and wives for each other, they got in touch with their own warmth and tenderness. The couples reinforced this by reflecting back to the priests the importance of their nurturing capacity. They experienced love from the people simply for being priests. They did nothing to earn it. For some, it was similar to a "falling-in-love" experience. They felt as if they were better men, more complete as persons. And they were. Their journey into the feminine, that is, their becoming aware of their *anima* for the first time or as never before, was opening a whole new world within themselves to enter and explore. (1987, 73)

Carl Jung described this same process of personal unification whereby one needs to integrate both the *anima*, or female side, with the *animus*, or male side. For Jung, personal fulfillment or individuation could not occur without this integration of the anima and animus.

Using Sexual Insights

Gallagher and Vandenburg take this concept even further by discussing how celibate priests can learn about the insights that married couples gain in their romantic and sexual involvements. They believe it is important for celibates to capitalize on the wisdom and insights of loving couples. They even go so far as to suggest that a priest identify a specific loving couple and ask them to draw up a series of guidelines a priest can use to see whether his life is indeed emotionally and spiritually fulfilled.

> Specifically, a priest could pick the holiest couple he knows who have a real grasp of their sacrament of matrimony and the dynamics of relationships. He would come to them for direction in terms of how he is living out his relationship with his people. Attention would not be on his ministerial skills but on his personal life, such as prayer, spirituality,

and how he approaches liturgies and homilies. The issue is not how well he does them but the mentality he projects toward the people when celebrating mass or giving a homily. What is his mentality toward women, brother priests, his bishop, or his blood family? Is he affirming of others? Does he show affection? Does he allow people to get close to him? . . . While many priests would be hesitant to try this, most priests would be surprised at just how perceptive some couples are and how helpful they can be in terms of relationship. But if love is present, there is no reason to fear. (1987, 121)

These guidelines help address many of the issues Patrick faced. When Patrick brought down "the wall," as he described it, between himself and women, he eventually realized that while he was intellectually progressing, he was emotionally cloistered. Like Gallagher and Vandenburg, he experienced the need to capitalize on the wisdom and insights that loving couples can provide.

Just as there are many ways of being sexual, there are also many ways of being celibate and of handling a religious commitment to celibacy. For some individuals, celibacy has probably been a way of avoiding their own sexuality and the development of their own sexual identities. For many others, like Patrick, their commitment to celibacy has evolved over a long period of time into a meaningful and personally rewarding commitment.

Using Celibate Insights

Just as many priests are becoming aware that they can learn from loving couples, many noncelibates may want to ask, what can we learn from them? Patrick spoke about how people can misuse sex for their own selfish purposes or simply for their own physical gratification. Since priests often contemplate and ponder what their celibacy means, shouldn't those of us who are sexually active do the same? Are we communing with our lover(s) and growing from our sexual involvement(s)? Are we enriching the lives of our lover(s)? Life without sex is complicated in a culture as eroticized as ours, but sexual activity can certainly become overly complicated pretty quickly. Perhaps this is the very reason some people choose periods of voluntary celibacy—to gain a more detached perspective on who and what they want to become sexually.

Patrick chose to become a celibate priest in pursuit of his dreams. Our next subject, Jennifer Bryce, chose to become a prostitute to escape her disastrous home life.

References and Suggested Readings

Bhaktipada, Swami. *The Joy of No Sex: How to Stop Worrying About AIDS and Start Living Happily Without Sex.* Moundville, W.V.: Palace Publishing, 1988.

Clark, Keith. *Being Sexual and Celibate.* Notre Dame, Ind.: Ave Maria Press, 1986.

Gallagher, Charles, and Thomas Vandenburg. *Celibacy Myth: Loving for Life.* New York: Crossroad Publishing, 1987.

Goergen, Don. *The Sexual Celibate.* San Francisco: Harper Religious Books, 1975.

Huddleson, Mary, ed. *Celibate Loving: Encounter in Three Dimensions.* Mahwah, N.J.: Paulist Press, 1984.

Kinsey, Alfred, Wardell Pomeroy, and Clyde Martin. *Sexual Behavior in the Human Male.* Philadelphia: Saunders, 1948.

Kinsey, Alfred, Wardell Pomeroy, Clyde Martin and Paul H. Gebhard. *Sexual Behavior in the Human Female.* Philadelphia: Saunders, 1953.

Knight, David. *Chastity: Who Lives It.* Albany, N.Y.: Clarity Publishing, 1985.

DISCUSSION AREAS

1. Even as a child, Patrick tried to win people's love and admiration by being extra helpful and good. Do you think his need to be good had a major impact on his decision to become a priest? Patrick's early sexual experiences and memories seem typical. Upon becoming deeply interested in Catholicism and the priesthood, Patrick adopted new definitions of his own sexuality. What impact has religion had on your sexuality? When Patrick became religious, he also began to feel guilty about his masturbation. What has influenced your feelings about masturbation? Do you think it is appropriate that many religions link guilt with masturbation?

2. Patrick's high school relationship with Shelly seemed like a typical first romance. However, because Patrick decided to become a priest, he established a wall between himself and his feelings for Shelly and for women in general. Are your career plans influencing your sexuality? Is your sexual behavior influencing your career plans?

3. Patrick limited his summer romance with Monica because he wanted to become a priest and also because he doubted her interest in him. Have you ever been in a relationship where you doubted the other person's commitment to you? How do we know who is likely to accept us romantically and sexually, and who is likely to reject us? How does our image of ourselves and of our romantic possibilities change as we grow older?

4. The marriage encounter weekend changed Patrick's life. During that weekend, he learned that men and women can grow emotionally through their sexual relationships. What have you learned about yourself emotionally from your relationships? What, in general, can men learn from women through intimate and romantic involvements, and is that different from what women generally learn from men?

5. Father Graddy's fraternity with the other five priests allows him to explore openly many emotional and intellectual issues. Do you think most men in our society have the opportunity for that kind of association with other men? Might such associations be a powerful way to learn and grow? Do women collectively explore these issues very often?

6. Tom's friendship proved to be pivotal in Patrick's life. In what sense is unqualified love an essential ingredient in most of our lives? As a celibate priest Patrick felt able to express his affection and love for Tom openly. Do you think many males are hesitant and fearful of showing their affection for another male? Do you think this is a major issue in our society?

7. Through our actions and values, we assign meaning to sexual activities. Clearly, for Patrick sex should be confined either to celibate love, as in his own case, or to a committed marriage. What do you see as the advantages and disadvantages to this system of sexual meanings? How does this system judge gay sexuality or premarital sexuality or masturbation?

8. Patrick believes that his life has a full range of sexual expressiveness, except for genital sexuality. Do you believe this is a reasonable demarcation? Do you think if you eliminated genital sexuality you would still have a full sexual life?

9. Suppose you found yourself in a situation where you were expected to live a celibate life. How would you react to this? What do you think influences the way you would react? Apart from religious reasons, why might one choose to be celibate?

10. There is an argument put forward by the Catholic Church that both priests and nuns, by forgoing sexual love for another person, develop instead a widespread love for their community and God. Do you think sexual love diminishes or enhances one's love for the community? Does sexual love diminish or enhance your spiritual capabilities?

11. Patrick expressed deep concern that sexual activity can be treated very casually and thereby become meaningless. Do you believe commitment is important to a strong sexual relationship? What kind of commitment is necessary in your opinion to build a solid, meaningful relationship? What kind of commitments have you had in your relationship(s) and how did they affect your sexual and emotional development?

12. Have your sexual relationships helped you integrate your *anima* and *animus*? Do you seek a lover who contrasts with or complements your basic personality?

6

A Journey into the World of Prostitution and Beyond: Case Study of Jennifer Bryce

Jennifer Bryce's long blond hair flows naturally well past her shoulders. Petite in stature, she carries herself well, and her smile and laugh reveal a cosmopolitan sense of humor. As an attractive woman with a quick wit and the natural charm of the girl-next-door variety, she does not conform to the stereotype of the heavily made-up, worn-out hooker. Yet Jennifer has ventured far into "the Life," as prostitutes sometimes describe their profession.

Born in the mid-1950s in Newark, New Jersey, Jennifer had a disastrous childhood. Her mother divorced her father shortly after Jennifer was born and remarried instantly. Jennifer had a stepsister, Clara, who was a year younger than she. Her mother and stepfather were well educated and held well-paying management positions, but Jennifer suffered at home.

She described her mother as a "party girl," and both her mother and stepfather had serious alcohol and drug addiction problems. Her mother had grown up being both physically and mentally abused, something she perpetuated on her daughters.

> My mother and [step]dad treated me pretty poorly. Lots of mental and physical abuse. I got a beating almost every day, sometimes twice a day. My parents were careful not to leave lots of marks. They would use a leather strap, or a wooden spoon, or sometimes they would just slap me around till they got tired. But the mental abuse was probably the worst. She would start in about how I or my stepsister were worthless, stupid, and no good. It was a mistake having us, it had ruined her whole life, and we would never amount to anything, and just on and on, and over and over, day after day. At three, those were my first memories, and this shit continued until I got put away at sixteen. I never felt safe—there was just no time out. I would be asleep in my bedroom, and at any minute the door would come crashing open, and I would start getting another beating. And she would hit me and yell, "You stupid (wack) son of a bitch (wack), good for nothing (wack), God damn you to hell (wack). . ." As a little

girl, I thought all girls got beat. You have to understand, those were my parents and the only life I knew.

Because of this unrelenting physical and mental abuse, Jennifer became very close to Clara. She loved Clara deeply and tried to protect Clara from the abuse they both constantly received.

I was the oldest, and I had a younger stepsister. Both of us got beaten. If Mom was real mad, she would beat us and then beat me again because I was the oldest. I tried to protect her some, but that would make Mom even madder sometimes. One day, Clara was very sick and so I asked her not to hit her. But she was awful mad, so after my beating, I got locked in the closet for a whole day, and after Clara's beating, Clara said she had to pee. Mom locked her out of the house, and when she wet herself and vomited, Mom beat her so bad that they could not send her to school for a whole week.

Surprisingly, even with this traumatic childhood, Jennifer assumed that her life was normal. The pain and emotional humiliation she suffered she repressed. She says even now, in her therapy sessions, she is only beginning to remember some of the worst of the things inflicted on her.

Many factors contributed to Jennifer's destructive childhood. Her parent's serious drug and alcohol abuse, their violent tempers, and their own unpleasant childhoods helped make them unfit parents. They were abusive to both children as well as to each other. Jennifer's early life had a surreal discord to it that she survived only by repressing her feelings. The family chose to remain socially isolated so she did not have access to peers to help balance her unpleasant family life.

Jennifer's early attitudes about sex were shaped largely by her mother.

I think my attitudes toward sex started with my mother. She would talk to me as a kid about how she hated men, how awful they were, and how my [step]father forced her to have sex most of the time. She really played up the victim stuff. This started when I was six, seven, and eight. And sure enough, I too chose to be a victim most of my life.

Being bright, Jennifer did well in grade school, and her teachers encouraged her academically. While her teachers suspected abuse at home, definite evidence was always cleverly concealed. During the early part of junior high, Jennifer began to be disruptive at school. With a marginal emotional life at home, Jennifer began clowning around and trying to win the attention and approval of her peers by any means at her disposal. At twelve years of age, she also began drinking heavily. Since she was able to steal pills from her parents she also developed a serious drug problem.

> At twelve, I started acting out at school. I got totally wasted on drugs and alcohol. I stole pills and booze from my parents. As I said, they were really into both. The way I drank and popped pills at twelve, I am surprised it did not kill me. I was curious and they both did it, so I tried it. And, wow, it was like I loved getting high and being wasted. Acceptance was always a big issue for me. At school, I wanted acceptance and to be part of the "in" crowd. If I had drugs or I drank, then I was one of the cool kids. And I would have sold my soul back then for acceptance. Unfortunately, all through my life I felt like I was never really accepted. I always had the feeling that I was on the outside looking in.

By age thirteen Jennifer felt abandoned by both of the significant men in her life. Her biological father disowned her for her drinking and acting out, after which her stepfather divorced her mother and promptly moved abroad.

Maturing and getting physically bigger, Jennifer began actively to resist her mother's continuing abuse. She began physically to defend Clara, who was considerably smaller, and she became violent toward her mother. During this time Jennifer had her first major experience with guilt.

> At fourteen, my mom and I would have at each other. My mom had divorced my stepfather by this time, and I was big enough to stand up to her when she started in on me or my sister. I remember one day, she threw something at me upstairs, and so I pushed her down the stairs. I banged her up pretty bad, and the police wanted to take me away. And then she used pills to try and kill herself. She was losing it, but I still felt massive guilt about that. You see, she had left a note saying how I had made her do it. And everybody knew what a rotten kid I had become. Incorrigible—that is what they called me.

Shortly after her mother's attempted suicide, Jennifer lost her virginity. She had met an older boy named Daniel who became her avenue of escape from her problems at home. She and Daniel spent a lot of time together, and these times were a reprieve from her oppressive home life. Jennifer and Daniel shared sex and drugs, since he too was a heavy drug user.

> I was still acting out when I started having sex. I had a boyfriend, Daniel, who was nineteen. I did not know much about sex. I had

never masturbated or anything. I just knew I wanted affection, and sex was what I could give to get it. And Daniel really wanted it, so I just kind of went along. I remember the first time we did it, I bled and I thought it was my period. So I got real embarrassed. I really did not understand much about it. And we continued to have sex pretty often, but I kept thinking, What is the big deal about this? It meant nothing to me, not bad, not good, but he did stay with me. When I was almost fifteen, I got pregnant. I had never used any kind of birth control, and he just dumped me. I waited three months to tell my mother. She was pretty cool, and since abortions were illegal in New Jersey, she took me to New York for one. I felt awful about that, but I could not take care of myself, much less a kid. I still feel so much shame about it [the abortion].

After her abortion Jennifer continued to have serious problems at home and at school. She had a number of transitory sexual affairs that meant virtually nothing to her. She slept around, trying to gain the attention and affection of the boys she knew in high school. Her drug usage increased, but since her unscrupulous uncle owned a pharmacy, her entire family had a steady stream of prescription drugs. During classes in high school she was often drunk, and twice she passed out during school.

Jennifer's first experience with prostitution occurred during a weekend visit with a friend in Providence, Rhode Island.

This man approached me in this bar. Like I said, I was young, attractive, definitely looked like a victim, and probably looked like I needed money. He offered me one hundred dollars to have sex with him. And it was like—oh people really do, do this! I just had not actually thought about it [prostitution] before. But I did it, and to tell you the truth, I have blocked off all of my feelings about that first time. I kind of remember what he looked like, but I do not remember the sex, getting the money, or any of my feelings about it. I know I did it, but I have blocked out that first time almost entirely.

When Jennifer turned fifteen, her mother decided to institutionalize her for her wild behavior and her drug and alcohol problems. Ironically, the mother saw Jennifer's drinking and drug problems as serious, while she continued to ignore her own. On her mother's orders Jennifer was sent to a therapeutic clinic called Integrity House.

It was what they used to call a therapeutic community. It was run by an ex-pimp heroin dealer, and it was like your worst nightmare. They shaved my head, they worked me twenty to twenty-four hours with only food breaks, and they used sleep as reward. If you followed all of their rules, then they would let you sleep one to two hours the first day, with an extra hour or two every day you followed the rules. Any screw-up, anything at all, and it was back to one hour of sleep. I wore a man's prison uniform with a sign around my neck saying I was an asshole. When they let us outside, we would stand at attention in the courtyard for hours. Their idea back then was to totally break you down. They broke your spirit, and when there was nothing left, built you up to follow their rules. I never felt more alone or more miserable.

Many of the frustrations and anxieties that Jennifer experienced at Integrity House were continuations of her earlier problems. In reflecting on this period, Jennifer felt her most serious problem was her increasing ability to ignore her own feelings. She felt that to survive, she had to repress all her feelings.

All through my childhood and even after I went to Integrity House, I really specialized in closing off my feelings. My family life sucked. I was desperate for attention, even negative attention. I constantly feared that I would be left, abandoned. I was always told by my mom and [step]dad that I was melodramatic, self-pitying, and just plain worthless. I survived. And I survived by closing off all my feelings. In the short run, it hurts much less if you totally deny your feelings.

While at Integrity House, Jennifer met Stan. Stan had major problems of his own, and he too was a serious drug and alcohol abuser. Stan and Jennifer formed an alliance that was to last for many years. After months of suffering at the institute, Jennifer, Stan, and another woman decided to escape. They broke out of the institute late one night and hitchhiked to San Francisco. Jennifer stole some money from her mother, and a friend in San Francisco helped the three of them secure a dilapidated apartment. But the three friends fell on hard times. Willing to do any kind of work for subsistence wages and for any kind of hours, Jennifer tried to secure innumerable jobs. However, since she was a sixteen-year-old runaway with no skills, no one would hire her. Week after week, she and the others tried unsuccessfully to find jobs. Their apartment near the North Beach area of San Francisco led them into constant contact with the drug world. Stan began selling drugs on the street, but he was not financially savvy, so even this did not help bring in much money. Frustrated, he became violent with both Jennifer and her girlfriend.

San Francisco at sixteen. Trying to find a job and nobody would hire me. No money and I got so hungry. Stan was a wannabe pimp, and he knew some girls who were out on the street. He thought it would be cool and we could make some bucks if I turned some tricks. And there was also some excitement about it—sort of like my chance to be bad—real bad. But when I actually got made up and out on the street, I was terrified.

Anyway, my first time with no pimp, I got strong-armed by a black guy who took me to a warehouse, violently fucked me, and then beat the living shit out of me. He took a telephone and hit me so many times in the face I thought I was going to die. He told me he wanted to kill me, and he beat me and repeatedly choked me with the phone cord till I passed out. Somebody found me and took me to the emergency room. When I became conscious, I told the doctor I had been raped. But some cop who was there just laughed and said I was just a dumb hooker who had not gotten paid. What he said hurt because it was true. The shame of it. It hurt to admit even to myself what I was doing.

When I got out of the hospital, Stan took me home and raped me. He did it as soon as we got to the apartment. He said he had to because I had to get over this bad trick. He said it was like falling off a horse and I had to learn to get right back on. I think it was then that I really started hating men. I never admitted it, not for a long time, but I really hated men.

After narrowly escaping being beaten to death, Jennifer left Stan and prostitution because she was so frightened. She lived in San Francisco on unemployment and by selling drugs and hustling money whenever possible. Stan eventually found her, and they became involved again. She also decided to go back out on the streets to turn some tricks. When asked why she became involved with Stan again, she replied, "I simply did not know any better. He was the type of guy I had come to know. I did not even know guys could be nice to you."

During this period Jennifer's drug usage increased. She would take absolutely anything to get high. Several years later, when checking into a drug rehabilitation clinic, she had to list how many different drugs she had taken during this period. The list included forty-six different drugs, plus alcohol. Often she would take several of these drugs simultaneously, and the overall effect was, as she described it, "just being wasted."

Just before her seventeenth birthday, she decided to leave Stan and San Francisco and go with another streetwalker to Provincetown, Massachusetts. Though Jennifer described Provincetown as quite an adventure, her actual life-style there was very similar to what it had been in San Francisco: she sold drugs, turned some tricks, and generally hustled money any way she could. The major change in Provincetown was the absence of Stan.

> Moved to Provincetown, or P-town, as we called it. I got to know lots of gays and bisexuals and just a wild sexual scene. I even went to the A-house—that is the sadomasochism bar with the famous back room. It is supposedly for exclusive leathermen, and at the time I was proud because I was one of the few women ever let in. What a scene—s/m, bondage, even one guy getting fist-fucked. We did a lot of wild stuff just to be wild. Another night I remember a New Year's Eve party at Piggies. Just before midnight, they locked the doors, four to five hundred of us got naked and danced. Some of my best friends were gorgeous, kept male prostitutes. I had my first lesbian experience there with a woman who had tatoos all over her face. She came on to me, and I let her do as she pleased. It was no big deal one way or the other. I also met some transvestites, guys who were simply beautiful. I used to be jealous of several of them because they were so pretty. All in all, P-town was quite a place.

During the year she spent in Provincetown, Jennifer did a lot of growing up emotionally. She developed a network of friends, including female and male prostitutes, transsexuals, and transvestites. At this time she also met a man named Mike, an exceptionally attractive man who had been earning his living as a male prostitute for homosexuals. Mike had an uncle who had died, leaving him a great deal of money. The only restriction on the inheritance was that Mike had to be married before he could receive it. Promising that he would support her, Mike asked Jennifer to move to Boston and marry him so he could secure his inheritance. Since she had made several bad drug deals, Jennifer thought Mike's offer sounded good.

The relationship with Mike proved to be a disaster. Like many of the men Jennifer had known, Mike was drug and alcohol addicted. One night, while extremely drunk, he tried to cut Jennifer's throat with a broken plate. She had him arrested and quickly moved away.

Again, to support herself, Jennifer resorted to prostitution. Later she began stripping, although within the trade the women always called themselves "exotic dancers" rather than strippers. Jennifer enjoyed "dancing." She was energetic and earned a great deal of money stripping. At only eighteen years of age, she would often earn $800–$1,000 a week dancing. With this income, Jennifer temporarily stopped turning tricks, because she "could now afford morals." She enjoyed the dancing and believed stripping was one of the ultimate female fantasies because women could excite men without having any real contact with them.

I got off on conning men as both a dancer and as a prostitute. It is always a twofold game where everyone gets to feel like they have the upper hand but where nobody really wins. In stripping, the guy says, "Ha ha, you bitch—I can make you bend down for a dollar," while the woman says, "Ha ha, you sucker—I just took your dollar and you cannot even touch me." That is the black and white of dancing. In prostitution the guy thinks, "Ha ha, you bitch. I can buy you for this amount of money," while the prostitute, who has to believe the act means nothing, just to survive, considers the trick a total fool to have to pay for sex. I think many hookers see life as a con game, and they think they are getting the last laugh or that they are above petty, conventional morality when they con a man into paying for sex when the sex means nothing to them.

As a dancer, Jennifer needed endless energy, and by using more and more drugs she kept herself going.

I was into drugs in a big way. Drugs kept reality at bay and helped make sure you did not have any feelings. Feelings were the enemy. You just got high to keep on trucking. You did not want to stop and think about what you were doing, and you never wanted to have feelings. Drugs were the escape from a lot of pain. You had to keep pretending. You had to push on. Drugs helped supply the energy to keep going.

As a dancer, Jennifer had to hustle drinks from the customers. Drinks ran eight to ten dollars, and the dancers were encouraged to get the men to buy champagne for fifty dollars a bottle. While hustling drinks, Jennifer became friends with a lonely man named Jake. Jake, who was fifty years old and a wealthy corporate executive from New Orleans, began to treat Jennifer as the daughter he had never had. He came to see her dance whenever he was in town and repeatedly told her that if she needed to get out of Boston and her life there, he would be happy to help.

Ultimately Stan showed up in Boston, and Jennifer, feeling the need to have someone care about her, began living with him again. Just as in San Francisco, Stan became dependent on Jennifer for drug money, and he resumed beating her. Also, at this time her heavy drug consumption began destroying her health, making her violently sick for weeks on end. She had to use drugs to keep dancing, yet they made her more and more ill.

Life in Boston got out of control. I was getting hassled by the police. I blacked out backstage one night at work. One of my roommates was dealing drugs and got shot at in a gay bar. She gave me a gun to carry "just in case," and Stan started wanting more and more drugs. Even though I would clear over a thousand dollars a week, it was not enough. He would get violent, and I was sick almost all the time now. I knew if I stayed, I would die soon. So I used my one means of escape. I ran off to New Orleans with my wealthy corporate friend and began to totally abuse his generosity.

Jennifer moved to New Orleans and began living with Jake in his large colonial house. Jake supported Jennifer while encouraging her to go to college. Jennifer always viewed Jake as the supportive father she never had and she never had sex with him, although years later Jake finally revealed that he did have a romantic interest in her. After two years of college, Jennifer met Bobby, another college student whom she found exciting. Because Bobby was extremely good-looking and had lots of girl-friends, Jennifer decided to pursue him. After several months she left Jake to move in with Bobby.

Bobby, another heavy drug abuser, taught Jennifer to inject drugs. She began to take increasing quantities of drugs, and mainlining them gave her more powerful highs.

Bobby and I lived in the [French] Quarter, and we partied a lot. At the time I thought we were perfect together. We were both into drugs and alcohol, partying, massively energetic—we just never stopped. We were rock-and-rollers, adventure-thrill seek-ers. Everybody knew about Bobby and Jennifer. There were parts of this relationship that were great. And when we got serious about it we even got engaged. But the drug and alcohol addiction was quite literally killing us both. Finally, I knew I had to try and stop.

Sex with Bobby was like her previous relationships. Jennifer never desired sex with Bobby, although she had chosen to be with him because he was so good-looking. Bobby initiated sex. Although she had orgasms and physically enjoyed sex, Jennifer never felt enough sexual desire to initiate it; instead, she simply responded to Bobby's desires.

As their thrill-seeking life together continued, Jennifer's drug depen-dency reached new extremes. She developed a vivid premonition that she was going to overdose and die in a shooting gallery (a place where IV drug users shoot their drugs together), and the only thing the other junkies would care about was how to get rid of her body before the cops came. Jennifer decided to seek serious drug therapy.

She had not been in contact with her mother since running away to

San Francisco, but she now asked her mother for help. She returned to New Jersey for therapy and joined Alcoholics Anonymous and Narcotics Anonymous. After five years of therapy, she also joined PRIDE, a support group for prostitutes and strippers.

> I finally realized that I had learned to become a fantastic sexual performer. The men I was with (and I was with quite a few) said I was fabulous. The thing was, I was not there—it was just an act. And I came to hate them because they never noticed. None of them really cared. And this hatred was like a major force which I only came to understand slowly through my therapy. Eventually I understood that this hatred of men was from being used by them. Then I finally realized I was doing this to myself, setting myself up to be treated like this. In AA and NA they helped me to start taking responsibility for the kind of life I was living. This was the real turning point in my life.

During her counseling, Jennifer began to face several of the recurring issues in her life. She therapeutically confronted her early childhood experiences, the violence that had occurred at home, her drug and alcohol problems, her prostitution and abiding anger toward men, and her overall repression of feelings which she used to survive. She explored her own victimization and began taking responsibility for changing her life.

Her therapy took two forms. First, she withdrew entirely from drug and alcohol usage. Second, she began to explore some of her inner, personal feelings and her extreme hatred of men. Her rage and anger at men led her into a sexual relationship with Lana.

Lana, a lesbian, actively sought out a relationship with Jennifer, and for the next two and a half years Lana and Jennifer lived together in an intense but problematic relationship. Lana was committed to the relationship while Jennifer was not. Jennifer thought she had finally discovered her true sexual identity as a lesbian. Joining the Gay Alliance, she felt that it was very important to "come out of the closet." She told all her friends and her mother that she was gay. However, she really did not intrinsically enjoy sex with Lana, and she began having fantasies about sex with men.

Jennifer felt that her relationship with Lana was better than being involved with a man whom she would probably come to hate. Later, her therapist said, "Jennifer, it is not that you love women, it is just that you hate men." This assessment by her analyst was accurate, for eventually Jennifer did decide she was sexually attracted to men.

After two more years of therapy, Jennifer tried to end her relationship with Lana, who turned out to be a most possessive lover. Jennifer finally separated from Lana after several violent confrontations. Shortly thereafter she met a man named Billy Bo who was the first man Jennifer felt she could trust. He was a friend first, later becoming her lover. Billy Bo was also a recovering drug and alcohol abuser, and they supported each other through two more years of AA meetings and outside therapy. At the end of two years, however, Jennifer felt that Billy Bo was still afraid of a truly intimate relationship, and she began to sense that intimacy was what she really wanted. Still confronting her anger toward men, Jennifer realized that she had put up many of the barriers to true intimacy. She had set herself up to be a victim, and that is exactly what had happened to her.

Knowing that she needed to change her life, she decided to move to Arizona, to live with Jim. She had known Jim for years, from Alcoholics Anonymous in New Jersey, and although he was ten years younger than she, they were close friends. Jim had joined AA when he was sixteen years old, and although he had not been subject to physical abuse as a child, he had been emotionally abused. He too came from a dysfunctional family and had a serious drinking problem by the time he was fifteen.

Jennifer has a different relationship with Jim: they share a commitment to stay away from drugs and alcohol. Seeking intimacy in their relationship, they are also excited about doing well in college.

Sexually, Jennifer's relationship with Jim is also different in several important regards. Jennifer has joined Sex and Love Addicts Anonymous and is again exploring her anger with men. Through her therapy she now feels she can express anger at Jim and that he will not abandon her simply because she has gotten mad. She is Jim's friend as well as lover. In her therapy she learned to set sexual boundaries for herself, and she does not have sex with Jim unless she feels like having sex with him. This is radically different for her because in all her previous relationships, she allowed herself to be sexually available to men on demand in order to secure their attention and affection. Now, for the first time in her life, she looks forward to sex and actually desires it.

> Prior to Jim, I was always in control during sex. I never let my feelings or emotions run away because then the guy would have control and power over me. I kept that power. Sure, I had orgasms, but I never let myself get carried away with those kinds of feelings. With Jim, I do not have to stay in control. I can let go. And that kind of intimacy and vulnerability is both frightening and exciting.

Jennifer and Jim still have many problems to overcome, both individually and together. But they remain determined to succeed. They spend a great deal of time and effort to be as open and honest with each other as possible.

Now in my life I have to really work to stay alive, healthy, and growing. I am in recovery not only from my addictions but from a life of hiding from my feelings and intimacy. I could go back to my addictions at any time. But now I know what life can be like, and I will do anything not to go back. I think I can make it now because I have someone I do not want to lose.

Jennifer is now determined to stay out of the world of drug dependency and prostitution. She does this not on moral grounds but with an awareness that those activities would ruin her new life. She and Jim have both been tested for AIDS and received negative results. Jennifer feels very fortunate because many of the dancers, prostitutes, and drug addicts she knows are infected with the AIDS virus or have already died from it. She feels incredibly lucky to have left this social scene because the emotional and physical toll it extracted almost destroyed her.

Her relationship with her mother is slowly improving, although she has been advised by her current therapist to "divorce" her mom. Her therapist believes a conscious severing (a "divorce") of her relationship with her mother would prove beneficial to Jennifer. However, she still wants to try to work things out. Recently she and her mother spent a lot of time reminiscing about the exploitive events of both of their childhoods. Jennifer sees Clara frequently, and they share a caring, supportive friendship.

Reflecting on her experiences, Jennifer feels there are several features of prostitution not commonly understood.

Prostitution taps into the unknown. It has an almost mystical quality to it because it represents an unknown life-style and so few people talk about it. It is also taboo—real bad stuff. People are fascinated by the undercurrents of society. People fantasize about relinquishing the sexual trappings which society puts on them, and prostitutes inhabit the underworld where the rules are openly, even wantonly, broken. Also, many people think that prostitutes, without society's restrictions, have learned tricks that they do not know, tricks which hold the secrets of sensual and sexual fulfillment. People think sexual fulfillment is based on some naughty trick or technique which uninhibited prostitutes must know. That kind of thinking is the basis of the myth and mystique.

Having been in that world, I realize we kept trying to promote that exotic mystique just to keep ourselves going. As street hangers, sure, we would taunt the tourists because we knew they were fascinated by us. But there was nothing that exotic about being all doped up and used. We knew underneath that far from real sexual wisdom, our real areas of expertise were loneliness, despair, and pain. Far from the exotic life, we were more like lost children. We had lost our way. And we just kept going by pretending, living to be hip, slick, and cool and never, never, never looking back.

Jennifer also talked about how power and issues of control played a major role in many of her paid sexual encounters.

The power trip is a big part of prostitution. Power is a big deal, oh yeah. This is especially true when they are dealing with overdominant wives, mothers, or when they are losers or submissive at their jobs. They can dominate this female because they pay for that, and the fantasy is on. They can be in charge. At least they can act that way for a little while. Also, a lot of these guys were just plain lonely. They wanted to talk about their girlfriends or wives, and because I was a paid stranger, they would tell me things they would never tell their wife or counselor or even their friends. It was heart-wrenching to me how many of these guys were fundamentally lonely. A lot of my customers were "suiters," guys in their three-piece suits. They have gone through their lives pretty dogmatically and they know what they wanted in a job, wife, and overall life-style. But so many of the "suiters" are wound pretty tight; they do not have many releases. But it is absolutely guaranteed that the guys in the three-piece suits are the ones asking for the really kinky stuff—lots of domination or humiliation stuff. They were the most repressed, but they were also the ones with the bucks.

Being just thirty-two years old, Jennifer has experienced a lot. She has lost the idealism and youthful enthusiasm typical of many of her college peers, but she has survived many traumas, and by surviving she has become determined to build a productive, loving life. In concluding, Jennifer had this to say about sexuality:

I think everybody should know how important it is not to run away from your feelings. I think it is healthy to take emotional risks, get close to someone. Sure, there can be pain, but is that worse than a life with no intimacy? I also think you have to be honest with yourself and to know why you are in a sexual relationship. You have to make sure that you are not setting yourself up to be a big loser. Sexually, we all need honesty, intimacy, the ability to forgive, and a sense of humor.

ANALYSIS

The Abuse of Children

The childhood experiences of Jennifer Bryce seem unbelievably painful. Many parents spank children occasionally, but actually to beat a small child is heinous. It is difficult for most of us who have not experienced that kind of environment to understand its impact. One of the most painful parts of Jennifer's early life can be seen in her description of how her bedroom door could come crashing open at any moment, with another beating following. It was interesting that, having no other basis for comparison, she just assumed that this was typical.

In his book *Healing the Child Within* (1987), Charles Whitfield emphasizes how important it is for abused or neglected children to confront their pasts therapeutically. Whitfield argues (as do many other therapists) that repressed childhood traumas negatively reassert themselves in adult behavior. Jennifer reached exactly the same conclusions.

Because of her dysfunctional and abusive home life, it seems logical for Jennifer to have sought desperately the attention of her peers. This problem was compounded by her easy access to drugs and alcohol. With her incarceration at Integrity House, she at last escaped her abusive home life. However, to escape her escape, she ended up putting herself on the streets of San Francisco. Desperate and hungry, Jennifer ultimately joined one of the few subcultures open to a young, unskilled woman on the streets—the subculture of prostitution.

Prostitution

Prostitution has certainly been around for a long time. Humorously labeled the "oldest profession," it has been a part of most societies in some form or another. Take ancient Rome, for example:

> Roman men attending sporting events in the local coliseums also found prostitutes plying their trade under the lower arches, or *fornices*, of the stadium. Their customers became known as *fornicators*. (Francoeur 1989, 256)

Winick and Kinsie (1971) did a study of prostitution in the United States by interviewing some two thousand prostitutes. They found that the social stigma of prostitution often attracts a personality type that is prone to drug dependency, and that many women become prostitutes to secure drugs. They believe that many prostitutes have pimps not primarily for protection, but through emotional necessity because of the demoralization inherent in the profession. This, they found, made the prostitutes overly dependent and vulnerable to pimps. This study also found that although society has the ability to conduct thoughtful programs of rehabilitation, it rarely does so because of social ambivalence and the low priority such programs usually receive.

Jennifer Bryce did not seem particularly prone to criminality, but she certainly was extremely dependent on Stan. Jennifer's progress in improving her life is due to her own determination, not to a well-funded or well-thought-out rehabilitation program.

Two more sympathetic treatments of prostitution can be found in Carmen and Moody (1985) and McLeod (1982). Carmen and Moody give an ethnographic account and an impressionistic description of prostitution in New York City's Times Square area. They present a bleak picture of prostitutes being victimized by almost everyone in their social environment: customers, pimps, drug dealers, police, lawyers, bail bondsmen, the courts, the media, and ultimately by society's moralistic stigma. Their sympathetic treatment of "working girls" includes their hope that society will move to decriminalize prostitution and remove much of the negative labeling currently used.

In *Women Working: Prostitution Now* (1982), Eileen McLeod postulates that women prostitutes are basically dealing with an economically disadvantaged position compared to that of men which can functionally lead them to sell their most salable commodity—sex. She presents pages of astonishing data to support her contention and then compares prostitution in the United States with prostitution in Britain.

While prostitution is legal in Britain (as it is in most of Nevada), soliciting is not. It is also illegal in Britain to be living on "the immoral earnings of another" (pimping), but there are still pimps in Britain, although they are called ponces. While McLeod's analysis does show that decriminalization of prostitution can create a more humane environment for prostitutes, many of the same problems arise.

> The women I interviewed asserted that the majority of prostitutes had ponces. The most frequently suggested percentage was 75%. A distinction was made between "heavy" ponces employing violence and intimidation and taking virtually all of a woman's money and men who were simply living off what a woman earned. All my informants agreed that "heavy" ponces were more prevalent for the women on the street. However, prostitutes working in other settings also had ponces. For example, women working in saunas [or clubs] commented that their colleagues were more independent of ponces than a few years ago but estimated that 60–70% of women in saunas had ponces of whom about 10% were "heavy." (44–45)

It seems reasonable to describe Stan as a "heavy" pimp, using this definition, particularly after Jennifer's first trick in San Francisco. Jennifer's case seems to fit the overall pattern found in the research literature on prostitution, except that her parents were well-educated professionals. Her parents' financial position had virtually no effect on her prostitution until she sought her mother's help for therapy.

Jennifer's case demonstrates that the life of a prostitute is invariably problematic. Even our cultural fantasies and myths about being "hip, slick, and cool" or about the glamorous life of the beautiful, well-paid call girl are unrealistic, particularly when compared with the reality that Jennifer and many others actually experienced.

Strippers

Two other aspects of Jennifer's story are worth reviewing. Jennifer described the excitement of stripping. In *Naked Is the Best Disguise: My Life as a Stripper* (1986), Lauri Lewin discusses how being a stripper allowed her to hide her actual personality while acting out the fantasy of the exotic temptress. Lewin's book also offers some parallels with Jennifer's statements on society's fantasies about sexuality, or what Lewin calls "sexual outlaws." Lewin maintains that society does have ambivalent feelings about sexual outlaws. On the one hand, there is the morally superior attitude: "How could any woman do that for money?" On the other hand, many males assume that sexual outlaws have transcended society's normal sexual restrictions and view them with a combination of apprehension and attraction. As Jennifer and Lewin know, reality is not really that simple.

Leather Sexuality, Sexual Extremism, and Sexual Pluralism

Jennifer also discussed visiting an exclusive leathermen's club in Provincetown. Geoff Mains, in *Urban Aboriginals: A Celebration of Leathersexuality* (1984), discusses how by being in "leatherspace" one can "escape the prison of the flesh." For the vast majority of us pain and humiliation are just not sexual. But leather sexuality and books similar to Mains's do stand as testaments to the incredible diversity of constructs evidenced in human sexuality and to the astonishing degree of sexual pluralism increasingly evident in twentieth-century America. What becomes sexual and who decides it is sexual is an interesting sociological process.

Battered Women

Before finishing the case study of Jennifer Bryce, it seems essential to deal with one final issue—why did an intelligent woman like Jennifer put up with Stan's violence and abuse? As mentioned in the case study of Libby Williams, some people form highly destructive, dependent (or, to use Peele and Brodsky's [1975] term), addictive relationships. In *Women and Male Violence: The Visions and Struggles of the Battered Women's Movement* (1986), S. Schechter exposes the shocking facts showing that many women are repeatedly battered. Often a family history of abuse, low self-esteem, no perceived options, and domineering males combine to form this unnerving scenario. What is remarkable about Jennifer is that she is determined to break out of this destructive cycle.

Jennifer has certainly suffered many different ordeals, but she is now choosing to move beyond these earlier traumas. She has taken responsibility for restructuring her life and developing an intimate and satisfying sexual relationship. In this we can only wish her the best.

Our next case study, that of Kevin Krammer, involves a middle-aged man who decided to change his life dramatically. He entered the realm of financial investment, becoming wildly successful and radically changing his self-image and his sexual life.

References and Suggested Readings

Carmen, Arlene, and Howard Moody. *Working Women: The Subterranean World of Street Prostitution*. New York: Harper and Row, 1985.

Francoeur, Robert, ed. *Taking Sides*. Guilford, CT: Dushkin, 1989.

Lewin, Lauri. *Naked Is the Best Disguise: My Life as a Stripper*. New York: Routledge Chapman and Hall, 1986.

Mains, Geoff. *Urban Aboriginals: A Celebration of Leathersexuality*. San Francisco: Gay Sunshine Press, 1984.

McLeod, Eileen. *Women Working: Prostitution Now*. London: Croom Helm, 1982.

Peele, Stanton, and Archie Brodsky. *Love and Addiction*. New York: New American Library, 1975.

Schechter, S. *Women and Male Violence: The Visions and Struggles of the Battered Women's Movement*. Boston: South End Press, 1986.

Whitfield, Charles. *Healing the Child Within*. Deerfield Beach, FL: Health Communications, 1987.

Winick, C., and P. Kinsie. *The Lively Commerce: Prostitution in the United States*. Chicago: Quadrangle, 1971.

Zausner, M. *The Streets: A Factual Portrait of Six Prostitutes as Told in Their Own Words*. New York: St. Martin's Press, 1986.

DISCUSSION AREAS

1. How would you have reacted to the extreme mental and physical abuse Jennifer suffered as a child? Do you think that many of Jennifer's problems later in life were caused by this traumatic childhood?

2. Jennifer's early attitudes about sexuality were definitely influenced by her mother. In what ways have your parents influenced your sexuality? Do you think parents' attitudes about relationships and sexuality influence one's overall sexual identity? What other factors have significantly influenced your sexual identity?

3. Jennifer reported the constant need in junior high and high school to be accepted, to be considered cool by her peers. She also reported that she always felt "on the outside looking in." Do you think Jennifer's poor family life led her to seek acceptance in high school? Do you think that, given Jennifer's traumatic home life, any other choice was possible? Are there ways Jennifer could have handled her youth better? What would you have done in her situation?

4. Jennifer clearly used drugs and alcohol in school to escape her personal problems. Do you think this is a common phenomenon? Do you think students use drugs and alcohol, and even sex, to try to establish their identity?

5. Jennifer did not use contraceptives with Daniel and became pregnant. There are over a million teenage pregnancies a year in the United States. Do you think most of these teenagers want to have children? Do most of these teenagers have adequate information about birth control? What factors have influenced your contraceptive behavior? What did you think about Jennifer's abortion? What did you think of Daniel's desertion? If you had been in her situation, how would you have handled this pregnancy?

6. Even before being sent to Integrity House, Jennifer had begun to ignore or repress her own personal feelings, simply to survive. In what sense do we all ignore some of our personal feelings? What do you think are the implications of ignoring our feelings? Do you think that for Jennifer this was an effective strategy to help her survive? The methods of resocialization at Integrity House were pretty extreme. What do you think could have been done instead to help Jennifer? Jennifer's repression of her feelings, particularly her anger toward men, seems similar to some of Libby Williams's early experiences. Do you think women in our society are encouraged to repress their anger? Is this a serious problem? What emotions are men encouraged to repress?

7. What did you think of Jennifer's long-term relationship with Stan? Why do you think Jennifer continued that relationship? While it is

easy to see the negative aspects of Jennifer's relationship with Stan, do you think Stan in any way helped Jennifer? Have you ever continued a relationship that was destructive? Why do people stay in such relationships?

8. Jennifer's first San Francisco experience at turning a trick as a sixteen-year-old almost led to her death, yet interestingly enough the most painful part of that experience (as related by Jennifer) was having the cop call her "just a dumb hooker who had not gotten paid." Why do you think that statement hurt Jennifer so much? How did you react to Stan's rape right after she was released from the hospital?

9. Jennifer talks about living in Provincetown as a sort of adventure. What were your reactions to the leather bars and the wild clubs that Jennifer described in Provincetown? Do you think we have too much or too little sexual freedom in this country? How did you react to the story of the sadomasochistic bar complete with the back room in which people can act out their sadomasochistic fantasies? Do you think this world of clubs is really all that exotic? Should consenting adults be allowed to do anything they want in a private setting?

10. In Boston Jennifer began stripping. She described the life of the stripper as one of the ultimate female fantasies—that of being able to turn on men without actually having to have contact with them. Do you think stripteasing is a prominent fantasy for women? What do you think are the power implications of striptease? Do you think stripteasing was particularly satisfying to Jennifer, given her background?

11. When Jennifer left Boston with Jake and relied on his generosity to support her through two years of college, she began to feel guilty. What do you think of her relationship with Jake? Do you think that in some ways Jake might have been the first person to provide some of the normal comforts that most of us find in our own families? Why do you think Jennifer left Jake to run off with Bobby and resume a life-style that she had said she wanted to abandon in Boston? How would you qualitatively evaluate Jennifer's relationship with Bobby? Many students report that they enjoy partying. What role do good times play in your intimate relationships?

12. When Jennifer returned to New Jersey and began counseling to confront some of her serious problems, she also began her relationship with Lana. How did you react to that relationship? Did you think it could ever have proved to be an effective way for Jennifer to deal with her extreme anger toward men? Many prostitutes end up seeking intimate sexual relationships with women. Do you think this is an acceptable strategy for female prostitutes who often resent men?

13. Billy Bo and Jennifer were both recovering from addictions. What did you think of their relationship? Eventually Jennifer realized that she

wanted more intimacy in their relationship than Billy Bo could handle. What level of intimacy do you seek in your relationships? How important is intimacy to you? Do you feel that many people avoid intimacy?

14. Jennifer's current relationship with Jim in Arizona seems qualitatively different from her earlier involvements. How would you assess their relationship? Do you think it is realistic to assume that they can build a new life together with intimacy? Jennifer spent so many years repressing her own feelings that currently she is having to expend a great deal of effort and energy to become more aware of her feelings. Though her case may be extreme, do you think many of us are discouraged from developing our own sexual and intimate feelings? Has this been an issue in your life? How have you dealt with it? Jennifer talked about not being able to "let go" during sex—not letting feelings of pleasure overwhelm her so that she could retain some control. Do you think this is an issue in many sexual relationships? Are you afraid or is somebody you know afraid of "letting go" in sexual encounters?

15. Jennifer's current therapist has encouraged her consciously to "divorce" and disassociate herself from her mother. Jennifer believes it is important to try to work out and resolve many of their early problems. Do you agree with Jennifer's plan or with the therapist's advice? Why or why not? How have you dealt with your parents when it comes to issues regarding your sexuality?

16. Jennifer discussed some social myths about prostitution. In one of her last statements, she mentioned that many people consider prostitutes more aware, more knowledgeable about sexual fulfillment because they do not respond to society's normal constraints on sexual expressiveness. Do you think social morality restricts our sexual awareness? Would you like to see society more or less sexually restrictive? What would be the implications of your changes?

17. After years of therapy, Jennifer described her sex life as a performance; the various men she had sex with felt she was fabulous, yet it was all an act for her. Are there performance pressures in your sex life? How do you deal with such pressures? Have you ever faked an orgasm? What would be gained by faking an orgasm?

18. How did you respond to Jennifer's last statement that "sexually, we all need honesty, intimacy, the ability to forgive, and a sense of humor" in relationships?

7
Radical Midlife Changes: Case Study of Kevin Krammer

Kevin Krammer, a balding, stout man, well into his seventies, might at first be mistaken for a slob. His extremely casual manner and overly faded jeans suggest an indifference to his presentation of self; the moment he speaks, however, his relaxed and articulate commentary alerts you to the fact that he is not only exceptionally well informed, but that his many years of experience have given him remarkable insights on everything from leveraged takeovers to open marriages. Though the language he uses regarding sexual issues seems dated, his awareness is not.

Kevin was born in New York City where he lived with his parents until college. His father was a successful corporate lawyer, and the family lived well. Being bright, Kevin always did well in school, particularly in art and in science classes. His natural talents in these areas would become a continuing theme in his life. His exceptional academic abilities allowed him to skip two grades by the time he graduated from high school.

Although precocious, Kevin had emotional problems, particularly with his peers. His only sibling (a sister five years younger) always wanted to play, while he preferred being left alone, usually to read or draw. Though never unpopular, Kevin often preferred being alone. He also wet his bed until he was almost sixteen years old.

When Kevin was eleven, his father quit his law practice to become a prominent figure in a multinational corporation. Also, because of Kevin's emotional problems and bed-wetting, his father sent him for psychiatric evaluation. Kevin enjoyed therapy and has continued growth-oriented therapy ever since then. Kevin liked being around his dad, who had significant business interests abroad, and the two of them traveled extensively together. With his father's support, Kevin excelled academically, but socially he remained isolated from his peers.

> I was very shy with women. I would say as a kid I was backward, socially. I did not get laid until I was twenty. I was under the impression when I was eighteen that, by golly, my manhood was at stake if I did not get laid. I was so shy and afraid of women that it was difficult for me to even know what to say or what to do. Finally, it became a major concern of mine, and I went out and did it. Later I wrote to a friend of mine who was at Brown

University and told him I got laid. He wrote back, "You bastard, how did you do that?" I do have a certain regret that I missed a lot with regard to my early sexual life. I have a sense that somehow I woke up very late to understand my own manhood and my own sexual capabilities.

After graduation from prep school Kevin did not know what to do. His father wanted him to enter the corporate world after gaining a distinguished business degree. His mother thought he should be a scientist. Kevin himself wanted to continue his painting endeavors, which had won some artistic recognition. He declined several college scholarships to begin painting full-time. During the next few years he achieved minor success with his paintings, which were well received at two uptown galleries. Finally, he felt that he was becoming an adult.

Well, everyone was bragging that they were doing it, but it was well known that it was bragging. The point is that back then, everyone believed that nice girls did not have sex. So it was a kind of very peculiar situation in which the girl you laid, you did not respect. There was that sort of double standard. It was okay to go out and do it, but if she let you, she was not worth going out with. Most of my early sexual experiences after prep school were very breast-oriented. You know, gotta get a feel. A bare tit was nirvana. I also did a lot of masturbating.

At nineteen, while still painting full-time, he became concerned about his virginity, which he felt made him less "manly." When Pearl Harbor was bombed, Kevin enlisted, but before going off to boot camp he visited a woman (named Kim) known to be "one of those women who would." Kim was kind and available, so he had sex with her for several weeks before he left for basic training.

Stationed in England during the war, Kevin met Pamela. Pamela was a "good girl" and a virgin whom he felt obligated to marry shortly after they became sexually intimate. By twenty-two he had married Pamela and his father had been killed in the war. Now Kevin felt he was growing up too quickly.

In many ways I was still just a kid. I loved Pamela, but we hardly knew each other. We helped each other grow up. I needed someone then. Everything just happened so fast. My dad's death hit me hard.

After the war he no longer thought seriously about a career in painting and art. Using his inheritance from his father, Kevin returned stateside with Pamela and bought a house near the university where he earned an undergraduate degree in chemistry. Though life felt secure and comfortable with Pam, Kevin began to sense that something was wrong with their marriage.

My first marriage, I would say, was basically a nonsexual affair. What I mean by that is I married my first wife because I respected and needed her. I admired her, but I was not sexually attracted to her. I just sort of felt that sex was not that important. I mean it was not that we did not make it. We did. But I was aware of not being terribly turned on. We were rather prim. Passionate sex was not something that I was even aware of.

How can I put it? I would go so far as to say it simply was a consequence of repression in my childhood of sexual matters which kind of continued in both our lives. I do not think she was terribly different than I was. We did it—we did not talk about it. There were times when I felt I really had to force myself, at least later in the marriage. We had trouble having children. I had a low sperm count, but we had them. I certainly have continued to masturbate into my adulthood. I love to masturbate. I have no qualms about it. . . . I like masturbation. I continued to masturbate. Very often in my first marriage, in particular, I masturbated instead of getting laid because I did not particularly like sex with her.

As he began his doctoral work in biology, Kevin did not know what to do with his marriage. He attended a nearby university, nationally known for its programs in the biological sciences, hoping that his graduate work would be the beginning of a new stage in his life.

Scientists are a kind of high priest in our culture. I wanted to do great research and be recognized as an outstanding scientist. I was pretty ambitious.

In pursuing his science career he felt the need to develop his professional image and be recognized. At this time his personal life and his relationship with Pam were "steady but boring."

By thirty-three, Kevin had finished his Ph.D. in biology. His work was published, but it was not considered outstanding. To advance further, he began a postdoctoral fellowship working in a lab with a famous biologist. In this lab he began to socialize extensively with the lab staff while Pam usually stayed home with the kids. At one lab party Kevin got stoned (on marijuana) for the first time and had sex with a co-worker. Although he had not been sexually involved with anyone since marrying

Pamela, this affair seemed like a grand adventure, even though the woman refused to continue sexually beyond this first encounter.

Meanwhile, Pamela found it difficult to understand Kevin's new lifestyle. When he told her about the affair she became distraught, and their relationship began a fatal deterioration, complete with increasingly poor communication and ill feelings on both sides. Within a year Kevin asked for, and received, a divorce.

> I was the one who wanted the divorce, but hell, it still hurt. I felt some guilt from my affair, but I felt even worse about how Pam and I had turned out. Our life together was like a mediocre friendship, and in terms of affection we had become more like brother and sister instead of husband and wife. For months I was depressed, hurt, angry, and terribly disappointed. Life seemed sour. Even the town I lived in felt more like an entanglement than a place where I could live vitally. I also missed having regular time with my kids. I suppose in some ways they have never forgiven me for leaving Pam.

At thirty-six, Kevin accepted an assistant professorship out West. The move helped him get away from his "Eastern entanglements." He published several papers and enjoyed his teaching and research. He also secured several research grants and organized his own lab. Socially, this was the first time Kevin felt like a "whole person and a functional adult." He became close friends with Robert, his new therapist. They traveled together, exploring various psychological growth centers throughout California and Oregon. His friendship with Robert was significant, particularly since Robert was Kevin's first close friend his own age. Sexually, Kevin became involved with several women.

> After my divorce and move, my real sex life began. Some of it was just for fun, some was very emotional. Throughout all of these relationships I was growing. I became a responsive lover and gained an awareness of many sensual possibilities. I learned about passion and how important that can be in a relationship. I also just had a lot of fun, which I think is a healthy dimension to feeling fulfilled as an adult.

At thirty-seven, Kevin started dating Rochelle, Robert's former lover. Rochelle, a music teacher in a junior high school, eventually became his second and current wife. Kevin developed a new maturity and intensity with Rochelle that he had never had with Pam. Kevin loved the passion he now shared with Rochelle.

As Kevin passed his fortieth birthday he began a serious reappraisal of his life. The recognition he sought as a famous scientist eluded him. Professionally he felt stagnated and trapped. The passion with Rochelle began to dissipate. He felt life was slipping away, so he decided to shake up his life by having an affair.

The affair with Zee was well beyond the bounds of what I would call reasonable. I think the primary driving force behind it was turning forty and going through a real bad midlife crisis. I went through a really bad one. In fact, I was abjectly unhappy for several years without really knowing what the source of my un-happiness was. I was feeling mortal: I could see my birth, I could see my death. I was on top of a hill, and everything was downhill from here on in. It was frightening, it was bewildering. I will even go so far as to say that I think there were chemical changes which took place in me. I cannot prove that, but I really felt like there were. For instance, I used to get up in the middle of the night and walk around the house crying. Sort of mourning my youth. I started writing poetry. I would break down and start crying after the slightest event. It was just a very emotional time for me. Also, my wife and I were going through a bad time together, so it was a compounded aggravation.

Kevin's affair with Zee proved to be another significant turning point in his life. Zee was more independent and sexually assertive than any woman he had known.

Zee, I would say, was one of the liberated women of this gener-ation. Namely, at the age of sixteen, she decided that this whole restriction on female sexuality was bullshit. She decided that she liked to fuck and that she was going to do it. I would say that her sexual attitudes were close to those of the traditional male. Let me amplify on that. I did not really discover this until we were into our relationship a little bit and I realized that this was something different. She was a very different woman than any other I had ever known. She was extremely selfish sexually. For example, she would "come" and then go to sleep. The kind of complaints that you hear from many women about their males are the kind of complaints I would make about Zee. She would only do it when she wanted it. She was very exploitative of men in the sense that she wanted sex from them, and she was pissed if she did not get it. She could be sensitive sometimes. I suppose she was looking for a relationship, but it had to be on her terms.

Sexually, Kevin's affair with Zee was the most intense and passionate he had ever experienced. Although he felt passionate with Rochelle, he had never encountered the kind of intensity he experienced with Zee.

> I just had never felt sexual energy like this before. We would have hard, fast, violent sex, take a shower, and start all over again. We kept going for hours on end, and as soon as we parted I would start getting hard just thinking about seeing her again. Mentally, I was totally obsessed with our eroticism. I felt like I was nineteen again, not forty-seven.

At this point Kevin really wanted to "have it all." To do this, he decided to continue his affair with Zee and simultaneously seek financial success. While he enjoyed the academic life and did not want to leave it, he wanted to make lots of money. The success that had eluded him as a scholar would be his financially. Using the last of his inheritance from his father, he carefully bought purchase options on nine large apartment complexes. With heavily leveraged venture capital, he converted more than five thousand apartments into refurbished condominiums. This quickly made him a multimillionaire.

Following his spectacular financial success, Kevin also told Rochelle about his continuing affair with Zee. His affair prompted his financial ventures, generating his wealth, which in turn gave him a new sense of confidence and purpose. He wanted to continue the affair with Zee while remaining married to Rochelle. To do this, he asked Rochelle for a sexually open marriage.

> This was a very energetic time of my life. The problems which I had experienced in my early forties and the sense of powerlessness which I felt vanished. My financial ventures were more successful than I had ever dreamed. My scholarship seemed to improve as well. The relationship with Zee was still intense, and yet I felt very close to Rochelle and my kids. For quite a while there, I thought I could have it all, and indeed my life seemed to prove that I could. Sexually, I never had more energy. Money and success really can be wonderful aphrodisiacs.

Eventually, Rochelle agreed to try an open marriage, in which extramarital affairs would be allowed and openly discussed. The first surprise under this new arrangement was Rochelle's sexual involvement with Jack, one of Kevin's graduate students.

> When she told me about Jack I was stunned. Suddenly an insidious double standard I had always had became very apparent.

While their affair continued, I suffered. It was hard being on the other side. I guess Rochelle's affair with Jack gave me new insights on what Pamela had gone through [when Kevin had his first extramarital affair]. I even took Zee to Paris for a long weekend, which she thought was most romantic. I was actually keen on leaving town then only because Jack and Rochelle planned on spending that weekend together.

Rochelle's affair with Jack changed her life in several unanticipated ways. Rochelle believed the experience helped her grow dramatically while allowing Kevin to experience some of the psychological costs involved in open relationships.

My relationship with Jack was important to me. We became good friends, and frankly I was quite flattered by his romantic interest. He was over ten years younger than me and most attractive in a rugged, manly way. I am not sure that our relationship was as sexual as Kevin imagined it, but I did want to please him sexually. He, on the other hand, enjoyed arousing me and I certainly moved beyond the routinized sexual patterns which had become so standard with Kevin and I. This was quite an adventure for me which I never would have had without Kevin's insistence on having an open marriage. I am not sure this really would strengthen most marriages, but it certainly helped mine.

Jack and Kevin developed problems, since Jack also worked in Kevin's research lab. Kevin described these problems by saying,

Having Jack in the lab was a bitch. Sure I was jealous, but having him around every day was like rubbing my face in it. I do not think he consciously tried to, but in many ways he seemed to flaunt it. Unfortunately, almost everyone in the lab knew about it.

While in many ways his life had never been better or more challenging, Kevin realized that what he really wanted was a committed and passionate relationship with Rochelle. When Rochelle's affair with Jack ended, she too became interested in solidifying her relationship with Kevin. After days of brutally candid discussion, Kevin and Rochelle decided he would end his affair with Zee, as part of the renewed commitment they were now making to each other.

On the last night that Zee and I spent together in bed, I was very sad. I told her I would miss her and I cried. I said to her that I knew I was not supposed to cry, but that I was just as unhappy as possible. We had a marvelous time together and I was going to miss her. I remember saying, "If I can let you see me cry, then anything else is all right." I always wanted to be totally open with her. Maybe I did that too late, but I would say we treated each other fairly. It was a good relationship that both of us will always remember.

Reflecting back on his relationship with Zee, Kevin said,

It made me feel good—it made me feel younger. It took the edge off of turning forty. It was a good thing—it really was. I do not regret it. What I regret, in hindsight, is the intensity with which I got involved with her. There were times when I contemplated getting divorced. I would say that the intensity of the thing with Zee did take energy away from Rochelle and therefore was something I should not have done to myself, or to her. But that is hindsight—that is what I learned. So I made some mistakes, but we have come through it. My marriage is stronger than it has ever been. There were some good things about it. I think it made my marriage more honest, even though it was a bitch for four or five months after Rochelle found out and during her affair with Jack.

For the last twenty years of his life, Kevin has found contentment with Rochelle. Life seems full, and he is particularly pleased that so many different dimensions of his life have coalesced.

I feel very fortunate in many regards. My life has come together quite well. I very much enjoyed being an academic at the university, but having a significant amount of money on the side certainly helped. The kind of financial asceticism that many faculty members have to live with, I find abhorrent. Money for me has translated into freedom, and I enjoy that freedom a great deal. I think that my first marriage and many of my sexual involvements have helped me grow up a great deal. As a young man, I was very shy and very frightened of women. In some senses, I simply did not grow much from my youth. However, by the time I was in my thirties I certainly did a lot more growing, personally, sexually, and professionally. For me, all of those factors have come together in my life in a way which I find very satisfying.

Kevin described the last twenty years of his life as the period in which he had been able to savor many of his earlier successes and achievements.

He enjoys traveling and his materially comfortable life-style. He spends a great deal of time with his children and has found them to be a major source of friendship and comfort in his old age. His relationship with Rochelle continues to evolve. Since they have shared so much, their relationship continues to be increasingly satisfying for them both. While their sexual activity has declined in frequency, Kevin does not feel any less passionate or interested in sex. He feels that over the years he and Rochelle have had traumatic times and committed times. Through all their differences, he feels they really have grown together through their varied experiences.

As a man approaching eighty, Kevin still has a vital and robust life-style. He objects vehemently when people begin to discount him now because of his age.

I think in our society it is easy to dismiss old people. They simply are not taken seriously. I find this quite aggravating because I feel I have never been more alert mentally. Even my position and money do not give me the kind of credence which they normally would. Let me give you just one example. Recently, after returning from a month's trip to the South Seas, I was talking to my son and I mentioned that it had been a particularly passionate trip for me and Rochelle. My son asked what I meant by that, and I just said that our sex had been very good. My son was appalled. He acted puritanical, although he certainly is not puritanical in his own life. He was shocked that I would even be having sex. I did not know what he really wanted me to do— just wither up and become an ineffectual old man? Well, I am not willing to do that for him or for anybody else either. Life is precious, and I intend to live every moment of mine as fully as possible.

ANALYSIS

Sexual Seasons

Kevin Krammer's life, though unique in many regards, follows the developmental stages discussed by Daniel Levinson and his colleagues in their book *The Seasons of a Man's Life*. As this book would predict, Kevin's life evolved through a relatively predictable series of stable building periods followed by transitional periods of change. What Levinson and his associates only briefly mentioned was that these predictable developmental periods or seasons definitely have dramatic sexual components.

In *The Eternal Garden: Seasons of Our Sexuality*, Sally Olds analyzes the sexual changes that the human life cycle usually includes. The professional issues Levinson and associates discuss she links in young adulthood with sexual explorations. The main point Olds establishes is that sexual turning points are very often linked to the overall changes, or seasons, occurring in one's life structure. For example, Kevin's divorce from Pam with its concomitant professional changes is what Olds describes as a common sexual turning point.

> One truth that has emerged from these tales of [sexual] turning points gives cause for optimism: very often a turning point that at first blush seems unrelievedly negative has turned out to have a happy ending after all. . . . The cataclysm of divorce, with all its pain, often leaves in its wake a strengthened individual personality and a never-dreamed-of sexual blossoming. (p. 10)

Open Relationships

During his next developmental stage, Kevin was married to Rochelle but he felt he was becoming a full-fledged adult with much more sexual passion than he had ever known. As this season evolved and his passion with Rochelle declined, he then became interested in experimenting with a sexually open relationship.

In their book *Open Marriage: A New Lifestyle for Couples* (1972), George and Nena O'Neill sparked much controversy by suggesting that a sexually open marriage offers potentials precluded by traditional marriages. The O'Neills emphasized that choice was the key to their concept of open marriage, and that open relationships give people the choice to become involved with new lovers and to grow emotionally from such involvements.

The O'Neills believe that monogamy can artificially restrict our personal growth. Later, Ulla and Richard Anobile wrote *Beyond Open Mar-*

riage in which they discussed the personal and emotional consequences of their open marriage, and how they became emotionally and then sexually involved with another couple. Eventually, this four-way relationship dissolved when one of the women left and they then formed a long-term ménage à trois. The Anobiles, like the O'Neills, argue that couples should at least consider other configurations for relationships beyond those traditionally associated with a monogamous marriage.

For some time there has been considerable interest among utopian writers about the possibilities of sexually open relationships. *The Harrad Experiment*, a classic once popular among undergraduates, told the story of a fictional college, Harrad, where undergraduates were randomly assigned to heterosexual living arrangements to see what kinds of personal experiences would result.

In the case of Kevin and Rochelle, it is clear that they believe that their open marriage was ultimately beneficial. The benefits they derived from this open relationship, however, had some heavy costs. Kevin's jealousy of Jack was certainly painful, and Rochelle's affair forced him to realize that an open marriage can have serious consequences. In his 1971 study "Swinging: The Exchange of Marriage Partners," Bell found that it was often the husband who was initially interested in swinging, although it was frequently the wife who ultimately enjoyed it more. This, in some ways, was certainly the outcome of Kevin and Rochelle's experiment in sexually opening up their marriage. It was not until Rochelle ended her relationship with Jack that Kevin and Rochelle were able to begin solidifying their own relationship.

Another interesting feature of Kevin's case is his continuing ambition to do better in terms of his personal relationships and his professional career. These ambitions seemed to be constantly intertwined. Nowhere is this interactive pattern more dramatic than in his financial success with the condominiums.

Kevin's statement that money and success were really wonderful aphrodisiacs is an interesting one to consider. In *Human Sexual Inadequacy* (1970), Masters and Johnson document the claim that loss of a permanent job is the leading cause of secondary impotence in males. So the idea that success and financial well-being promote increased sexual energy has a flip side: loss of a job or financial problems can easily promote impotence and sexually dysfunctional behavior.

Aging and Sexuality

Being nearly eighty years old, Kevin now has to deal with society's attitudes toward the aged and their sexuality. As his last remarks show, he is concerned that older people are often denied their right to be sexual in whatever way they deem fit. In *The Social Forces in Later Life,* Robert Atchley documents that although there are some physiological impairments that can negatively affect sexual performance in old age, most sexual problems experienced by the old are actually cultural or psychological in nature. Atchley maintains that sexuality is not a problem for most older people, even those who are eighty or ninety, if they continue to be active sexually. He reports that with advancing age, being sexually inactive for several months causes some men to lose their ability to achieve orgasm. This often happens after a spouse's death when even masturbation stops.

Edward Brecher reports in *Love, Sex, and Aging* that 84 percent of married people in their fifties are happily married, and that proportion rises to 88 percent of those in their sixties, and to 91 percent for those over seventy years of age. The two major factors reported as causing this marital happiness were good communication and sexual sharing. The most interesting figure in the Brecher study was that 95 percent of the happily married couples in the fifty- to ninety-three-year-old group reported a high level of sexual enjoyment with their spouses (p. 274).

This research clearly indicates that sexuality can be and often is an important part of life for many older people. There is also considerable evidence that older people resent the social intolerance of their sexuality (as discussed by Kevin). Here is one of the more humorous attempts to address this sexual intolerance toward the aged:

> Bill Baldwin, an East Lansing industrial consultant, decided to change the image of older people. Baldwin is the publisher and one of the models for a calendar featuring nude men and women who are all in their sixties. The oldest is sixty-eight, and he has sixteen grandchildren. Baldwin says finding volunteers for his enterprise was not a serious problem. When he published his first calendar in 1982, he solicited buyers to send along photos and suggestions for the 1983 edition. He received 187 nude self-portraits.
>
> Why produce such a calendar? Baldwin responds: "We didn't go along with the popular image of senior citizens: loneliness, laxatives, and Social Security. We intend to hang on to a significant place in life, physically, financially, emotionally, and sexually. We wanted to make that point, but we didn't want to be too solemn about it." (Kart 1985, 88)

More recently, some people have begun to insist that old people should become more sexual. An edict of this type, however, can be just as annoying and demeaning as the more traditional approach of denying older people their right to be sexual.

> Perhaps more than any other aspect of life, sexual behavior is subject to cultural regulation. Societies set standards for what is sexually desirable and undesirable, normal and abnormal. The current cohort of older peo-

ple grew up in periods of restrictive guidelines regarding appropriate sexual behavior. They are now faced with new values, often dictated by the mass media, of openness and freedom of sexual expression.

Older persons are told that sex is great exercise and an antidote to insomnia, depression, and loneliness! Yet *this new ethic of openness can be as difficult to live with as the more restricted sexual dictates of the past.* It may unduly pressure older persons, who were raised during more puritanical periods, and in whom references to sexuality may arouse feelings of shame and guilt. In *dealing with older people's sexuality, practitioners need to be sensitive to their clients' values and to support them making their own choices about sexual behavior and sexuality— even if these contradict what is currently in vogue.* (Hooyman and Kiyak 1988, 307)

Ultimately, it seems that society is often determined to make arbitrary and potentially devastating decisions about how people should express their sexuality. We have seen this in the other case studies as well. It seems humane to let adults choose for themselves a pattern of sexuality that makes sense to them, as long as they do not exploit others or flaunt their activities. Yet all too often we direct and even dictate specific sexual behavior that we as a culture consider appropriate, regardless of the individual's needs and desires. In this sense, our culture is erotocentric, and by being erotocentric we try to limit severely each individual's choices and options for sexual fulfillment. One wonders why the idea of a sexually pluralistic society is so alarming and threatening to many people.

Power-Sexuality

In reviewing his life, Kevin said he did a lot of growing personally, sexually, and professionally and that all these factors came together in a way that he found very satisfying. Kevin (like other subjects interviewed) found that when his sex improved so did his professional life, and vice versa. For Kevin, developing his sexuality also helped him grow and seek new professional challenges. Power-sexuality is the process whereby people like Kevin use positive sexual experiences to empower other dimensions of their lives.

While Kevin's life was basically one of positive changes, our next subject, Ed Fogelberg, has had to reshape his life to deal with his AIDS infection. In Ed's case study, we will see just how complex and socially volatile homosexuality and AIDS can be.

References and Suggested Readings

Anobile, Ulla, and Richard Anobile. *Beyond Open Marriage.* Roanoke, VA: A & W Publishers, 1979.

Atchley, Robert. *The Social Forces in Later Life.* 3d ed. Belmont, Calif.: Wadsworth, 1980.

Bell, R. "Swinging: The Exchange of Marriage Partners." *Sexual Behavior* 1:2 (1971): 70–79.

Brecher, Edward M., and the Editors of Consumer Union Books. *Love, Sex, and Aging.* Boston: Little, Brown, 1984.

Hooyman, Nancy, and H. Asuman Kiyak. *Social Gerontology: A Multidisciplinary Perspective.* Needham Heights, MA: Allyn and Bacon, 1988.

Kart, Cary S. *The Realities of Aging.* 2d ed. Needham Heights, MA: Allyn and Bacon, 1985.

Levinson, Daniel, Charlotte Darrow, Edward Klein, Maria Levinson, and Braxton McKee. *The Seasons of a Man's Life.* New York: Ballantine Books, 1978.

Masters, William, and Virginia Johnson. *Human Sexual Inadequacy.* New York: Bantam, 1970.

Olds, Sally. *The Eternal Garden: Seasons of Our Sexuality.* New York: Times Books, 1985.

O'Neill, George, and Nena O'Neill. *Open Marriage: A New Lifestyle for Couples.* New York: Evans, 1972.

Rimmer, Robert. *The Harrad Experiment.* New York: Bantam, 1978.

DISCUSSION AREAS

1. Kevin had problems with maturing during his childhood. His bed-wetting continued until he was almost sixteen, and he was inept and shy, particularly around women. What factors in our lives influence our level of maturity? What factors influenced your maturation? How do you think these factors affected your sexuality?

2. Kevin talked earlier about "getting laid." He even spoke of how he felt the need to "get laid" with his wife. While some men continue to speak of sex that way, do you think this need to "get laid" is more a phenomenon of Kevin's generation than of young people today? What sort of sexual pressures exist today for young people? Do you think being a virgin is a difficult role for a young person today? Did you feel pressure to become sexually active?

3. Kevin talked about how, when he was growing up, women were either good or sexually active. Do you think some of this duality exists today? Do you think women still have to face an either/or choice in defining who they will be sexually? Do men and women face different kinds of sexual pressures?

4. Kevin and Pam married young. She had been a virgin, and he felt obligated to marry her because she, a respectable woman, had chosen to become sexually involved with him. Do you think this was a sound reason for getting married? Do you think that even today some people feel they should get married simply because they have started having sex? How did you evaluate the quality of Kevin's relationship with Pam? Can a relationship be both dynamic and secure? Have you been more interested in security or dynamic qualities in your relationship(s)? Why?

5. Kevin was certainly ambitious. Early in life, he wanted to be a "high priest scientist" and later he was determined to be financially successful. How do you think his ambition influenced his relationships? Do you think his relationships influenced his level of ambition? How do you see these two concepts being related in your own life?

6. Even though Kevin chose to divorce Pam, he still experienced a great deal of pain and suffering. In some ways, it was not only the relationship that he had chosen to end but also the dream of a fulfilling and worthwhile marriage. How do ideals affect our relationships? What happens to our hopes at the end of a relationship? Do you think we see our relationships more realistically after they are over? Kevin said, "After my divorce and move, my real sex life began." Why do you think many people experience a major sexual rejuvenation after a relationship or marriage ends? Why do we often feel more

sexual energy as a new relationship begins? Must long-term relationships by their very nature become predictable and less exciting sexually? Have you done anything in your long-term relationships to help keep them sexually enlivened?

7. At around age forty, Kevin had what is frequently labeled a midlife crisis. He had to figure out who he was, what he wanted to become, and how to face his own limitations and mortality. This crisis affected both his personal relationships and his professional aspirations and goals. How do you see yourself developing both professionally and personally? Do you think Kevin's crisis was all that unusual? Do you think you will be confronting these sorts of issues at midlife?

8. Kevin's relationship with Zee seemed to be part of his midlife crisis. As a sexually assertive woman, she represented a kind of lover Kevin had not encountered before. Do you think most men are comfortable with an independent and sexually assertive woman like Zee? If you are sexually active, who initiates sexual contact in your relationship? Does this pattern of initiation reveal anything about you or your lover?

9. Kevin's financial success certainly gave him new options. Interestingly enough he reported that financial success was a wonderful aphrodisiac. What role do you think success and financial achievement play in our intimate lives?

10. How did you react to Kevin and Rochelle's open marriage? Do you think their open marriage helped them? Would you ever consider having an open relationship? Why or why not?

11. Kevin was quite jealous when Rochelle had her affair with Jack. Rochelle even said, "I am not sure that our relationship was as sexual as Kevin imagined." What role does jealousy play in your life? Do you think jealousy can be a productive emotion, leading to positive changes in a relationship? Do you think Rochelle used Jack to win back Kevin? Rochelle also reported that she was flattered by the attentions of a younger man. She herself was probably experiencing many of the same midlife crisis issues that Kevin was facing. Do you think taking a significantly younger lover often helps people deal with issues of aging? Is part of your own sexual image being able to attract young, good-looking sexual partners? Do you think this will change as you grow older?

12. Kevin finally decided to end his affair with Zee. Do you think this was fair to Zee? Should she have guessed this might happen, as it often does in affairs involving married men? What role do you see honesty playing in your intimate involvements? Is it important in your relationships to be able to plan a future together?

13. As he grew older, Kevin became concerned that our society and culture discount older people. Do you see this as a serious issue? Kevin also became concerned that even his own children had a hard time dealing with him as a sexually active person in his late seventies. Do you think many people find it hard to accredit the sexuality of older people? Do you have a hard time accepting the sexuality of older parents or grandparents? Do you just ignore this? Why do you think these problems occur? For you, is there something inherently threatening or alarming about the sexuality of older people?

8

A Life of Contrasting Options:
Case Study of Ed Fogelberg

E ven in a crowded room you would probably notice and remember
Ed Fogelberg. You would spot him quickly because he loves to
talk, and, being witty, he has a humorous response or joke for
absolutely every situation. While Ed is of average height, with a ruddy
complexion, he is thin. He has lost thirty to forty pounds in this last year.
As an energetic and personable thirty-five-year-old, Ed now faces life as a
gay man living with the challenge of HIV infection. (Human Immunode-
ficiency Virus [HIV] is the virus known to cause AIDS, which is the last
stage of long-term HIV infection.)

Born in Detroit, Michigan, Ed has three sisters and one brother. With
his father in the army, Ed described his early life as that of a typical army
brat. The family moved frequently, and the children, while all close, were
overly well behaved because their father was very strict with them.

> My father was quite the disciplinarian. In fact, while he was in
> the army he got nicknamed "The Warden." My mother was much
> more easygoing, philosophically, although in practice she ac-
> quiesced to my father's style out of fear. In many ways she was
> afraid of him. My parents lived amicably together for many years
> but not really lovingly. On some fundamental level I know my
> mother really does not love my father.

Ed's father withheld all affection toward his children and even explained once that "he did not have a duty to love us kids—he just had
to love his wife." Another powerful theme in Ed's early life, in addition
to that of an unloving and authoritarian father, was his attraction to
Catholicism. Even as a small boy, he went to church and was deeply
moved by the religious activities and rituals. Religion has always been an
important part of his life.

The most significant event in Ed's early childhood occurred when he
was ten.

> When I was about ten my dad started drinking heavily because
> he did not get promoted when he thought he should. It really
> changed his life. He decided he had a lousy family, a lousy life,
> and nothing was going right for him, so drinking became his only
> means of escape. My childhood ended at that point because my
> dad just sort of gave up on the family. Housework, yardwork,

taking out the trash, washing the cars—all that became my responsibility. He just came home and drank. He told me it was time for me to become responsible, that it was time I grew up. He hated it when I played with the other kids. I think it was really more an issue of his drinking and down-on-life attitude. Also, the man has no sense of humor or playfulness—everything is serious to him. As Dad got deeper and deeper into his booze, Mom went out and got a job and became the strong, dynamic woman he had never allowed her to become.

Ed's father continued his drinking and withdrawal from the family; with his mother frequently at work, Ed spent most of his free time with his brother and sisters. Ever since early childhood, Ed has remained emotionally close to his siblings and mother.

He remembers even as a small child having open and candid discussions with his mother about sex.

From what my mother says, my father needs sex frequently. At one point I remember her saying that she just wished it would fall off. My mother is a person with a low sex drive. She lived most of her adult life feeling like she had to put out to avoid his wrath. I think she put up with sex just to keep our family together, at least until he became a full-time alcoholic, and then she went out and got a job. She always felt she did not have any other options.

In his early teens Ed began masturbating. The sex education program at his junior high was limited.

In junior high school we received little tidbits of information about sex, not much information really. As a matter of fact, I thought you could get syphilis from masturbating—that is how much they were educating us. I think they gave us just enough information to scare us. They told us you could get diseases from sex, and I knew masturbation was sex, so I began to wonder what diseases I had. Anyway, I went to the public library and got all the books I could find on sex, and none of them said anything about masturbation causing syphilis. It's ironic now that I was so worried about masturbation.

Also in junior high, Ed began feeling physically attracted to other males. At this age, he did not know anything about being gay.

In junior high, of course, I heard the terms *fag* and *queer*, but I never even heard the terms *homosexual* or *gay* until I was in college. Of course, growing up I had physical attractions to male classmates, but I dated girls. I dated a lot of girls, and that was fun.

Even in high school Ed continued going out with girls.

In high school I did a lot of dating. Eventually, I was going steady with this one girl, and it reached the point of heavy petting. We did everything except have intercourse. That, of course, was to be saved for marriage. It was really enjoyable, and I think I ended that relationship. After that I never had a real girlfriend again. I do not think there was any one event or moment when I realized I was gay. I had inclinations about being attracted to men for a long time, even as a kid. I thought some of it might have been searching for a father figure since my own father was not much of a role model. I also remember in high school some of the guys caught Tom Dean beating off in the bathroom at school. All of us used to call him "Tom Dean the screaming queen." We knew he was different, and we ridiculed him for it. So I guess even in high school, I really had not understood my own gayness.

By the end of high school Ed has strong sexual feelings for other men; nevertheless, living in a society that basically condemns homosexuality, he continued to try to be heterosexual. This pattern continued for several years. However, after high school, his main interest became religion.

At nineteen Ed decided to enter the seminary to become a priest. Ed explained his decision by saying, "I went to the seminary because I thought I had the calling. I felt I was called by God to go into the service of the Church."

The seminary did not prove fulfilling for Ed. He enjoyed many parts of the religious life, but he felt the seminary lacked the social and sexual options he now wanted. Before leaving the seminary, he learned more about being gay and made his first homosexual contact.

In the seminary I first heard the term *homosexual*, and I came to know what it meant. Then one of my roommates told me he was gay, and I just took that in stride and left it at that, but about this same time I thought about experimenting with it just like I had experimented with straight sex. Shortly thereafter, I left the seminary because I did not want to be a priest. The idea of celibacy was not that appealing. Then, my roommate was dismissed from the seminary, and one night at his house we decided to experiment. It did not do much for me. I was really terrified. The whole concept of sex frightened me. Then I joined the army, met Jim, and we went even further down the road of sexual experimentation.

Ed really disliked military life, as he had lived it with his parents. Yet upon leaving the seminary, he joined the army because it was a familiar and readily available option. As he continued to develop his own sexual identity, religion temporarily became less important in his life.

Jim and I were good friends. He was, by his own admission, a practicing homosexual and he said he wanted to practice on me, so we did. We had both oral and anal intercourse. He was a good friend. It was not romantic or anything; for me, there was no combining romance and sex. As a matter of fact, just prior to getting involved with Jim, I went out with another army buddy and we procured two [female] prostitutes. I had sex without an orgasm. At that time I still wanted to try some straight stuff.

Ed did well during his first months in the army. Being bright, he advanced rapidly and was ultimately put up for a top secret clearance to work in intelligence. During the clearance investigation, the army discovered his homosexual encounters, whereupon he was honorably discharged from the army. This experience led him to conclude that indeed he was gay.

After the investigation, when they found out I had been sexually involved with men, I was honorably discharged on psychological grounds. During this process, I decided to tell my mom that I was gay. I thought about developing this long, drawn-out conversation that would take many twists and turns, eventually bringing up homosexuality and finally my own sexuality. When she walked in the room, I just blurted out, "I want to tell you I am gay"— so much for the big buildup! She stopped and thought about it and was fairly accepting. She did ask if I wore dresses and stuff. She was relieved to know I did not. Later, she had some guilt about where she went wrong, but eventually she even saw through that. She said that once she thought about it, she realized I was not a different person than the one she had raised and loved. Her only regret to this day is her lack of grandchildren.

Since both the seminary and the army had proved unsatisfactory, Ed did not know exactly what he wanted to do with his life. Even his sexual identity remained somewhat confused. After being honorably discharged,

Ed drifted around Denver doing various odd jobs. This was an unsettled and disturbing time in his life. Even attending church daily did not help much. Eventually, he became a waiter at a fancy restaurant.

All the waiters hung out together. Even on our days off we would come in to the restaurant and hang out at the bar. We all partied together, and when some of them started going to the gay bars, I would go too. At this point I found out I was really turned on to other men and that they were turned on to me. I had a lot of one-nighters and what we call fuck-buddies, those being friends who I had sex with. It was almost two years later that I had my first boyfriend, my first affair, but this period at the restaurant was important to me. I was accepted. Gorgeous men found me attractive and interesting. It was during this time that I really started enjoying life.

By the time I was twenty-three, I was having a wonderful life, and I finally had my first real relationship. I think that in many ways I was afraid to really get involved, but then I started seeing this guy who was not much of a threat because he had a [regular] lover. Lots of gay men are.home wreckers. They sleep with their friends who have lovers and some of it is pretty casual, so Dan and I started having sex, and surprise, surprise, it turned into a relationship. He really helped me a lot with my self-esteem. Funny thing was Dan's lover knew Dan and I were having sex. This rather confused our friends because I would go out with the guy I was seeing regularly one night, and then the next night I would go out with Dan, and the very next night I would be out with Dan's lover, who I eventually started having sex with. Finally, Dan started going out on us both a lot, and I spent quite a few nights with Dan's lover in a bar somewhere where we would see him out with his new boyfriend, although later that night he would come home to one of us. I really loved Dan, but now I am only friends with his lover. Dan dropped out of both of our lives. When I see his lover I always tease him about "his friend" [meaning Dan], and he always wants to know if I have heard from "my friend" [meaning Dan]. It is a sort of comic-tragic humor which we still share.

For the next five years Ed was active in the party circuit available to gays in metropolitan areas. Spending lots of time in gay bars and discos, he developed a large circle of friends, acquaintances, and lovers.

After several years working as a waiter, Ed became a loan officer at a bank, but his social life remained centered within the gay party circuit. He now spent busy days in the banking community and his nights at the gay clubs. Through all of these changes, Ed maintained a steady interest in religion. Ultimately, he decided that his spiritual interests deserved more of his attention.

During my real partying years I was also trying to work on my relationship with God again. In my partying I kept pushing God out of my life, but I would still go to mass every day. I lived almost right behind the main cathedral, so I would come home from the bank, go to mass, and then change [clothes] and go out to one of the clubs. I do not think it is incompatible to be homosexual and Christian; I have never had guilt over that. I guess I just believe in a forgiving God rather than a punitive one. By twenty-eight I think I wanted to focus more on my spiritual side rather than putting the emphasis on partying, so I finally decided to go to a monastery. My friends all laughed and said I would be busy [sexually] there, but it was not like that at all. I gave up the hunt and chase.

Ed left Denver, banking, and the gay club scene to enter a Missouri monastery. There Ed found his life calming down again, particularly socially, and he felt that he matured through his faith in God. He also learned some important lessons.

One day in the monastery I received a very simple but powerful lesson. I got angry because I had to labor outdoors in the heat while several of the other novices got to do light paperwork in the air-conditioned office. When I told my superior this was not fair, he replied, "Why, life is not always fair, but it is still wondrous." I do not think I fully understood the wisdom of that until I realized I had AIDS several years later.

Although Ed felt that his time in the monastery helped him mature, he again realized that the sheltered life of a cloistered monastery did not suit him. Late in 1984 he left the monastery, seeking a life where he could develop spiritually and still have a sexual life. At about this same time Ed first heard of a new disease called AIDS.

In 1984 when I left the monastery everyone started talking about this new disease, AIDS. We heard about this disease in San Francisco that was killing gay people left and right, but I thought, Well, that is a long ways away; besides, nobody I know has the disease. I felt perfectly safe. AIDS would never affect me.

After leaving the monastery, Ed lived with his parents while deciding what he wanted to do. Several months after returning to his parents' home in southern California, he had his first major AIDS-related illness.

After leaving the monastery, I moved in with my parents because I had no money. I found an Episcopal faith community that was really alive. After just two meetings people were calling me by my first name. They invited me into full participation in their community life. Then I came down with mononucleosis, and I started having heavy night sweats. Every pore I had would open up, and sweat would simply gush from my body. I slept on bath towels which would be soaked in the morning. I lost thirty-five pounds in two weeks, and although no tests were available early in 1985 I started thinking I might have AIDS.

Ed recovered from his mononucleosis, and though he had some minor infections, he did not have any serious diseases for the next two years. While working at a bank again, he became quite involved with the Episcopal community. He relished the new combination of professional activities and immersion in this religious community. However, he kept coming down with varied infections, which ultimately led to his being diagnosed as HIV-positive.

I kept coming down with little infections here and there. After the HIV tests were developed, I went to my physician to deal with these infections, and he said, "Do you want to take the [AIDS] test?" I said no, no, no, because I think I knew I had it. I really did not want it confirmed. I did not want to face up to this disease.

About a year after the first tests were developed, I came down with pneumonia; I simply could not breath. The X rays confirmed my pneumocystic pneumonia, and my doctor insisted that I have the [AIDS] blood test. Ten days later I went back to his office; his nurse told me I was positive [on the test]. Oh wow, I felt like I had just been given a death sentence—my whole body felt the fear.

Upon learning that he had been infected with the HIV virus, Ed entered a period of tremendous shock and anger, alternating with fear and depression. He now knew he might die quite quickly, and he had to learn to live with that knowledge. Though it was extremely difficult to deal with this news, his mother and one of his sisters provided much comfort.

My mom knew I had had the blood test, so she and my sister found out the same day I did. So at least ever since I found out I have had a support group. My sister even told her fiancé that she loves me and is going to stand by me even though I am gay and have AIDS. He understood and is still with her. At first everyone in my family knew except my father. He was not an easy person to tell. I think that I am extremely lucky to have kept my family through this. I have friends who were completely shunned when their families found out they had AIDS. Some people can be unbelievably cruel. One of my friends who was shunned by his family finally died. When I called them to say he had died, they told me they did not care. I know I do not want to die alone.

With anguish, pain, depression, and fear intruding, Ed had to decide how he would live his life as a person with HIV. One of his first decisions was to live as best he could without searching for someone to blame.

I do not know who I got the virus from. Knowing where it came from does not matter to me, and it hardly alters the real point, which is that I am infected. I know that none of my friends would have knowingly spread this. So my anger at having AIDS was directed at myself, God, life itself, and my situation rather than being focused on some pointless witchhunt.

In his quest to deal with AIDS, Ed began to educate himself on the physiological aspects of this recently discovered disease. At the same time, he decided to forgive himself rather than blame himself for what had happened.

When I was first diagnosed, I had a 39-CD4 cell count. The CD4 lymphocyte count indicates how prepared the body is to fight infections. A normal CD4 count is between 600 and 800. Now, two years later I am down to 22. I probably should not even be alive today, from a medical perspective. I think my faith in God is keeping me going. Also, I do not carry around a lot of anger. That would be a big drain. I have even forgiven myself for the things I have done in the past so that I can make the most of the time I have left.

Ed also had to decide how being infected with the HIV virus would affect his sexual life. He fairly quickly came to the following decision:

I do not want to be a murderer. When I die I do not want to go before my maker and explain why I continued to have sex with the HIV virus and, in doing so, committed murder. There is only one way to absolutely ensure that I do not pass this on to another, and for me that means never having partnered sex again. I know some PWAs [persons with AIDS] who say that a sexual shutdown is just a phase after you find out you have it. Some of them think latex condoms with Nonoxynol-9 are enough protection. Sometimes they do not even tell their partners they are infected; and, of course, many HIV-positives do not even know they are carriers. But for me, I know, and I have stopped having sex. It is the only way I can handle this.

As time passed, Ed began to wrestle philosophically with the knowledge that he had this devastating disease. This contemplation ultimately changed his life in several positive ways.

Most people go through their life feeling immortal. One's own death is very much an abstraction to most people. With my HIV-positive diagnosis I had to experience and grow from my own mortality well before I was old. For me life itself has become powerful. Sunsets seem more colorful; I hear birds singing now which I never remember hearing before. Everything takes on more meaning, knowing it can all end so soon. A person with AIDS, marked, as it were, with death, has the chance to appreciate the infinite wonderfulness of it all.

During the next two years Ed restructured his life, becoming a counselor at an AIDS outreach center. He became actively engaged in helping other people with HIV. His focus within the community is to help educate people about the spread of HIV and to help sensitize others to the human dimensions of this terrible disease.

After four years of living with full-blown AIDS, Ed attended a national conference on AIDS.

I met an intense new friend, Tad, at a national conference on HIV. One afternoon Tad asked me why I had put away several important issues—like why I was now ignoring my own sexuality and why I had not told my father about being infected. I suddenly realized that I had been ignoring these issues. I realized that I still had sexual feelings which I was ignoring and that I did not have to live in fear of my father any longer. Tad helped me face those issues and even though I never had sex with him, he did reawaken that whole sexual side of me which I was totally repressing.

After returning home from this conference, Ed decided that for his own peace of mind he wanted to tell his father about being gay and infected with the HIV virus. Even though his mother thought this was a bad idea, Ed proceeded anyway.

> I felt a tremendous weight lifted off my shoulders after I told my dad. Finally I have nothing to hide from him; everything is out in the open now. I expected him to throw me out of the house and never speak to me again, but he did not. He still has a hard time dealing with it, but he is trying in his own way. And there is a lot less pressure in my life now. Something my doctor and I were both surprised about happened within a week of my telling Dad: my CD4-cell count doubled to 34! Not very high but still an improvement. I was surprised that my psychological relief in telling Dad would have a noticeable physiological impact.

After telling his father, Ed became sexually active again. His initial fears about being a murderer by knowingly infecting someone else were replaced by his emerging awareness of safe sex procedures and his desire to live sexually again.

> There is safer sex. It is possible to be sexually involved with some-one without transmission of any body fluids. You do not have to have intercourse. I have learned to share myself sexually and to receive sexual satisfaction and pleasure without putting another or myself at risk. I have even avoided reinfecting myself with a different strain of HIV in the one sexual encounter I had where my partner was also a PWA. I am glad that I am again dealing with my own sexuality and sexual needs. I love hugging and kissing and mutual masturbation. Foreplay can be fantastic, a secret many heterosexual men do not appreciate. I love being sexual and intimate again.

Ed felt more contented and less anguished as a PWA. He talked openly and compassionately about dying, and he began helping his family deal with his impending death.

> I think I am ready for death. I have spent a lot of time putting my life in order. I hope I do not have lots of pain before I die. I really do not want to be drugged to the point where I do not know what is happening. I do not want to die, but if it comes, I am ready. My mother still has a hard time talking about the big "D," but we are making some progress. I told her I did want to make some plans about my funeral, and she asked why I would

not leave it to her. So I said, "Knowing your taste, I do not want to be caught dead in some of the stuff you would pick out." She really did not know whether to cry, laugh, or hit me.

Ed believed that while the HIV virus poses many unique problems and challenges, at least now there are innumerable agencies and support groups available to help.

People who are accurately diagnosed HIV-positive today do have some things to be thankful about. They are not the first to go through this, and there are good support groups now available. There are a wide array of caregivers available, with more emerging every day. They should also know that many of us have shown that AIDS is not such a horrible thing. One should not give up on life. No one's family should stop loving. Also, many PWAs go through the steps Kübler-Ross describes in her book *On Death and Dying* (denial, anger, bargaining, depression, and, finally, acceptance). Except for PWAs, instead of mourning for another you do it for yourself. But my point is, there are many supports and supportive people to help you live with AIDS as fully as possible.

There is the National AIDS Hotline, which can help you contact support people in your area: 1-800-342-AIDS. There is also a hotline operating at the PWA Coalition Newsline (1–800–828–3280). Both groups have information about local agencies and support groups. Local agencies can provide financial support, housing and food assistance, spiritual-emotional support groups, peer counseling, family counseling. Some groups are even opening up hospices as alternatives to the more standardized hospitals. There really are enough support groups such that any PWA can find some help. Shop around—there is a lot of variety in these groups. There is no longer any reason to be an outcast and suffer alone.

There are many different faces to HIV infection, and Ed used his situation to help educate others who may be at risk. He advocated an AIDS test for anyone who is sexually active or uses intravenous drugs.

Even though I was not eager to be tested for HIV myself, I would recommend such tests for those who are sexually active. Even in a monogamous relationship one of the partners could have been infected previously. If you contract HIV, the sooner you are diagnosed, the sooner you can receive medication and generally the longer you will have to live—I mean that is the selfish reason.

Altruistically, if you are infected, you need to do some serious rethinking about your sexual relationships.

In dealing with PWAs, community support groups, and the general public, Ed believed it is important to understand how the terminology of AIDS actually affects the self-esteem of PWAs.

I like the term *PWA* (person with AIDS) because in many ways we are not passive victims. Some like the term *person living with AIDS*, but some of us are not living very well emotionally or physically. For me, *PWA* delineates us first as people and secondarily as people with the AIDS virus. *PWA* is fine as long as it is not used to reduce a person into a simple category or thing. I do not view myself simply as a gay man with AIDS. I see myself first as a human being, then as someone with a serious disease.

Ed continued speaking to all kinds of people in his HIV education efforts. Sometimes while speaking he has been confronted by hostility, even hatred.

During some workshops I have been yelled at and told, "Faggot, why don't you just go away and croak." And that is okay. I understand the fear and hatred which some people have. Getting people to understand the human dimension to this disease is not easy. I suppose as it affects more and more straight people and more and more people die, there will be more understanding. It is a shame that it will take so long and require such a heavy price.

This trauma of HIV has allowed Ed to put his life together in new and enriching ways. He feels his work in the community and his outreach efforts have given his life a new meaning and a dynamic, integrated sense of purpose. He feels that his life is better than ever before, and that in some powerful ways having HIV has integrated his social work, his belief in God, and his overall outlook on life. Ed does not want to die, but planned to live his life enjoying each and every day.

Ed believed that it is important not to ignore the AIDS issue, and he had this to say for those who are currently sexually active:

A lot of people out there think that we are talking about AIDS too much. I simply do not agree. There are a lot of knotheads out there who simply believe that they could never get AIDS, that this could never ever happen to them. Sure, when AIDS first spread it was almost exclusively gays and IV drug users, but that too is changing. We are beginning just now to see more and more heterosexuals at the support centers. I predict *before this is over*

EVERYONE will know someone who has died from AIDS. I only wish that all of the people who are not currently infected but who are sexually active would take this danger seriously and take steps to prevent it from spreading further. We can prevent this from spreading and we must.

Ed realized his mission to help educate others about HIV even more dramatically when he ultimately became ordained as a Deacon in the Episcopal Church. His special calling, as the Bishop announced, would be to help the HIV positive as well as all of the affected. This extraordinary achievement was Ed's way of blending his contrasting options.

Twelve weeks after becoming a Deacon, Ed died of several opportunistic infections that his weakened immune system could not fight.

Recently, there has been some encouraging medical news regarding new options that appear to slow the progress of HIV infection, AIDS, and even HIV-related deaths. Monotherapy of AZT (a HIV-fighting drug) in the late 1980s has given way to combination antiretroviral therapy (drug cocktails) including a new class of drugs such as the protease inhibitors. If this trend continues HIV/AIDS may be treatable more as a chronic infection to be managed despite the fact there is still no cure. Research into a vaccine has continued, yet with more than a decade of testing, an effective vaccine still eludes us.

All of this encouraging news is tempered by the latest statistical reports showing that the spread of HIV continues systematically in the U.S. and explosively in much of the Third World.

Right now we have all the knowledge needed to stop the spread of HIV. Knowing this, Ed's final plea that we must stop the spread of HIV remains as valid today as it was when he was alive.

ANALYSIS

The case of Ed Fogelberg's life contains two distinctive sexual dimensions: homosexuality and HIV. We will consider these sequentially. With an authoritarian father and a retiring mother, Ed had early developmental experiences that were fairly typical. However, beginning in junior high school and continuing through his discharge from the army, Ed began to realize and accept being gay. This process was not particularly easy for him.

Research on Homosexuality

Alan Bell and Martin Weinberg, from the Kinsey Institute, completed an extensive study of homosexuality that was presented in their epic book *Homosexualities* (1978). Since many of their major findings bear directly on the case of Ed Fogelberg, we shall summarize them here. First, Bell and Weinberg studied the variety of different gay life-styles, concluding that even the very term *homosexual* is misleading because there are so many different ways homosexuals live.

> While the present study has taken a step forward in its delineation of types of homosexuals, it too fails to capture the full diversity that must be understood if society is ever fully to respect and appreciate the way in which individual homosexual men and women live their lives. (p. 231)

Clearly we must not ignore the diversity of gay life-styles, for to do so would be like equating Father Graddy's sexual life-style with that of Nick Orren. To avoid being provincial, and since the majority of us are heterosexual, we need to understand both the variety and complexity evident in gay life-styles. Fortunately, there are many interesting and thought-provoking novels and plays available. Christopher Bram's *Surprising Myself* (1988), Harvey Fierstein's *Torch Song Trilogy* (1978), and the eminently readable and humorous *The Object of My Affection* (1988) by Stephen McCauley are all highly recommended.

In addition to documenting this diversity of gay life-styles, the Bell and Weinberg findings also contradicted several well-established gay stereotypes. They found that contrary to the research findings of Laud Humphreys (1975), most homosexuals (ignoring the important variations already discussed) are *not* socially or psychologically maladjusted.

> It is difficult not to agree with the conclusion that homosexuality is a sexual variation within the normal range of psychological functioning. Many [homosexuals] could very well serve as models of social comport-

ment and psychological maturity. Most [homosexuals] are indistinguishable from the heterosexual majority with respect to most of the nonsexual aspects of their lives. (p. 148)

Bell and Weinberg agreed with the earlier Kinsey reports that homosexuality-heterosexuality is a continuum. In this sense, the very terms *heterosexual* and *homosexual* are misleading.

Homosexuality-heterosexuality is not necessarily an either or proposition. Rather, people can be distinguished on the basis of the degree to which their sexual responsiveness and behaviors are limited to persons of a particular sex (male or female). (p. 53)

As you remember, Ed had a number of heterosexual experiences, including one with a female prostitute. Yet, without ignoring the existence of this continuum, and recognizing the inherent limitations of labels, it seems fair to say that Ed was a homosexual, since he was primarily attracted to men.

Causes of Sexual Orientation

In another extensive study done by the Kinsey Institute, *Sexual Preference: Its Development in Men and Women* (Bell, Weinberg, and Hammersmith 1981), the researchers concluded that we do not know exactly what causes sexual orientation. The researchers did find that by adolescence, most people have developed a sexual preference that continues throughout their lives, and that, typically, homosexual behavior emerges several years after a person has distinct homosexual feelings/attractions. Most homosexuals (men and women) have had some dissatisfying heterosexual experiences. In this sense, one is not gay just because one has not tried heterosexual activities, nor is one gay just because such experiments prove dissatisfying; one is gay because one has homosexual feelings and attractions.

The researchers also found evidence to expose another common myth: that weak fathers and domineering mothers cause homosexuality. Identification with either parent does not appear to play a significant role in sexual orientation, although slightly more gay sons and daughters did have greater difficulty relating to their fathers when compared with heterosexuals. This last finding was seen as an outcome not a cause of sexual orientation (Bell, Weinberg, and Hammersmith 1981).

Ed's case aligns with these research findings. Though no one knows conclusively what causes homosexuality (or heterosexuality), it seems unlikely that Ed's relationship with his father or with his mother had any significant bearing on the development of his homosexuality. Ed tried heterosexual activities, and yet by adolescence he began to sense his basic attraction to men.

The Future of HIV/AIDS

In 1994 a groundbreaking new study by Edward Laumann and associates called The National Health and Social Life Survey (NHSLS) was completed, using a truly randomized sample of the U.S. population (something Kinsey did not have for his research). The researchers stated in *The Social Organization of Sexuality: Sexual Practices in the United States* that after a careful analysis of mathematically modeled American sexual networks HIV is *not* likely to spread dramatically into the heterosexual population.

"We are suggesting, however, that the general lack of connectivity present in sexual networks among adults in the United States, together with relatively low transmission probability of AIDS through vaginal intercourse, will significantly restrict the extent to which this disease will spread into the general population" (Laumann et al., 1994, p. 282).

A word of caution is in order here. The researchers are not saying that heterosexuals will not continue to get infected with HIV. What they are saying is that because most Americans have so few sexual partners this majority of the population is really at low risk. However, individuals with many sexual partners or STDs obviously will continue to be at risk.

The good news from this dramatic research report is that the U.S. probably will not have the carnage of HIV deaths found in many Third World countries that have sexual networks with much higher numbers of sexual partners. In the U.S. a growing concern is the spread of HIV through IV drug users and their sexual partners. Since HIV lives in the blood, sharing IV drug needles is highly dangerous. *People using IV drugs or with experienced sexual partners still need to use safer sex techniques.*

Social Responses to HIV/AIDS

The social history of society's response to AIDS is quite complex. Randy Shilts has written a fascinating review of America's reaction to AIDS in his book *And the Band Played On* (1988). Shilts maintains that American society ignored or minimized the AIDS crisis simply because it initially affected only gays and IV drug users. He makes a powerful case that it was not until the death of Rock Hudson and the Reagans' involvement with his death that we as a society began to mobilize significant efforts for research and education. It was not until 1988 (and even then some objected) that the surgeon general, C. Everett Koop, mailed the *Understanding AIDS* brochure to every American household.

As of June 1998 the CDC reports that over 400,000 Americans have died of HIV complications. This is more than seven times as many American deaths as in the Vietnam War. An increasing number of AIDS support groups have become available. In addition to the national resource centers that Ed mentioned, there are many community-based organizations that now have specific programs to help PWAs, their families, and friends. The national organizations can help identify local support agencies.

Paul Monette's *Borrowed Time: An AIDS Memoir* (1988) is helpful in understanding AIDS on the individual level. In this book Monette gives a stirring account of his life as a person with HIV. Christopher Davis documents his view on AIDS in *Valley of the Shadow* (1988), sharing how his lover died from AIDS-related diseases and how he is now living with the disease himself. His account includes powerful, sometimes painful insights, but like Ed he still retains his sense of humor. A number of practical AIDS caregiver handbooks are also available. Two of the best are Ted Eidson, *The AIDS Caregiver's Handbook* (1988), and Leonard Martelli, Fran Peltz, and William Messina, *When Someone You Know Has AIDS: A Practical Guide* (1987). With this kind of background, it is easier to understand Ed's encouraging words for those diagnosed as HIV-positive.

Ed's life shows two very powerful themes: his interest in God and religion, and his learning to develop and express his emerging homosexuality. We saw that neither the wild, gay party life nor the monastic life was entirely satisfying for him. Interestingly enough, becoming infected with the HIV virus seemed to encourage him to pull his life together, integrating his religious beliefs with his role of helping others deal with AIDS. His life has been full of transitions, and in some strange and interesting way, the HIV virus inspired him to make the most of those transitions.

Some qualifications, however, need to be made. HIV has many faces. Just as it is wrong to assume that there is one way of being sexual, it is equally naive to assume that Ed's HIV infection and ensuing reaction are typical. Ed has had an unusually positive attitude and physical reaction to HIV. The following selections show how others have reacted. Billy Howard, a noted photographer, took sixty-eight photographs of people with AIDS, asking them to write an "epitaph" under their photo to share their experiences as PWAs with the rest of us. Here are four of their statements:

My mother gave me a surprise birthday party for my 30th birthday. She wanted red candles on my cake, finding them after going to three different shops. I didn't even notice that there weren't any candles on the cake. Later, she told me that when it came time to put the candles on the cake that she decided against it. She thought that some of the people wouldn't want me blowing on the cake. It has been especially difficult for me being a woman.

—Deb (subject 7), Atlanta, Georgia, July 1988.

In the midst of illness, rejection, isolation and probably death—out of the darkness—hands reaching out—not family, friends or lovers, but strangers loving, caring, giving of themselves—they have renewed my faith and are my strength. I love you.

—Roy Griffen (subject 6), Atlanta, Georgia, March 1987.

Dying from AIDS is hard enough. Living with it is even harder.

—Drew Carroll (subject 46), Washington, D.C., May 1988.

I have made my choice, "I'm sitting tight until there's a cure. Then as soon as a cure is found, I'm going to drop dead from the excitement." With love—

—Kenney Taub (subject 48), New York, New York, May 1988.
(Howard 1989)

Ed Fogelberg has managed the transitions in his life productively. Our next subject has not been so fortunate in this regard. Terry Grant's case documents the life of a famous rock and roll star whose professional success was coupled with serious drug abuse and total sexual estrangement.

References and Suggested Readings

Gay Readings

Bram, Christopher. *Surprising Myself.* Fort Worth, Tex.: Owl Books, 1988.
Fierstein, Harvey. *Torch Song Trilogy.* New York: Gay Presses of New York, 1978.
McCauley, Stephen. *The Object of My Affection.* New York: Washington Square Press, 1988.

Interesting Research on Homosexuality

Bell, Alan P., and Martin Weinberg. *Homosexualities.* New York: Simon and Schuster, 1978.
Bell, Alan P., Martin Weinberg, and Sue Hammersmith. *Sexual Preference: Its Development in Men and Women.* Bloomington: Indiana University Press, 1981.
Humphreys, Laud. *Tearoom Trade: Impersonal Sex in Public Places.* Enlarged ed. Hawthorne, N.Y.: Aldine De Gruyter, 1975.
Laumann, Edward, J.H. Gagnon, R.T. Michael, and S. Michaels. *The Social Organization of Sexuality.* Chicago: University of Chicago Press, 1994.
Tripp, C.A. *The Homosexual Matrix.* Utica, N.Y.: Meridian, 1987.

HIV/AIDS Readings

Davis, Christopher. *Valley of the Shadow*. New York: St. Martin's Press, 1988.

Eidson, Ted, ed. *The AIDS Caregiver's Handbook*. New York: St. Martin's Press, 1988.

Feinburg, David. *Queer and Loathing: Rants and Raves of a Raging AIDS Clone*. New York: Penguin Books, 1994.

Howard, Bill. *Epitaphs for the Living*. Dallas, Tex.: Southern Methodist University Press, 1989.

Koop, C. Everett. *Understanding AIDS*. A publication of the U.S. Department of Health and Human Services. U.S. Government Printing Office, 1988.

Kübler-Ross, Elisabeth. *On Death and Dying*. New York: Macmillan, 1970.

Martelli, Leonard, Fran Peltz, and William Messina. *When Someone You Know Has AIDS: A Practical Guide*. New York: Crown Publishing, 1987.

McLennan, Rob. *Written in the Skin: A Poetic Response To AIDS*. Toronto, Canada: Insomniac Press, 1998.

Monette, Paul. *Borrowed Time: An AIDS Memoir*. San Diego: Harcourt Brace Jovanovich, 1988.

Shilts, Randy. *And the Band Played On*. New York: Penguin Books, 1988.

DISCUSSION AREAS

1. One stereotype holds that ineffective, weak fathers help create homosexuality. While there is no research evidence to support this conclusion, Ed's alcoholic father certainly did not help much with his role modeling. How much of an effect do you think Ed's family situation had on his sense of identity? Did your early family life influence your self-image?

2. Ed mentioned that his mother was a person with little sexual interest and that his father wanted sex frequently. How important do you think it is that a couple have approximately the same interest and level of sexual desire? Do you see your own level of sexual desire as relatively fixed? What influences or changes your desire for sex? Our image of contemporary American men is that, like batteries, they are sexually "ever ready." How realistic is this notion?

3. In junior high, Ed heard the terms *fag* and *queer* and began, with many of his friends, to make fun of and deride homosexuals. Ironically, Ed turned out to be gay. Do you think adolescents are particularly intolerant of sexual variations? Do you feel that as an adolescent you were fairly intolerant? How did you deal with people around you who did not follow mainstream heterosexual life-styles?

4. In high school, and even later in the army, Ed dated women because of social expectations. He began realizing he was not sexually interested in women but instead was interested in men. However, it took him until his mid-twenties to realize fully that he was gay. How long do you think it takes most people to understand who and what they want to be, sexually? Do you think this process slows down by the age of thirty or forty?

5. When Ed met Jim in the army and began "moving further down the road of sexual experimentation," he was developing his own sexual identity. What sorts of things have you done to develop your sexual identity? What kinds of experiences have you had or do you think you will have that could be pivotal in establishing your sexuality?

6. Though honorably discharged from the army, Ed decided to tell his mother he was gay. How do you think your parents would react to hearing that? While most of us are not gay, we all have sexual issues we do not discuss with our parents. Do you think it is important to let one's parents understand the basic parameters of one's sexuality? What issues would you never share with your parents? What sexual issues do you share with your friends? Do you share different issues with your men and women friends?

7. When Ed began hanging out with other gay waiters, his overall satisfaction and his sense of who he was sexually changed dramatically.

What events in your life have influenced your sexual development and either increased or decreased your enjoyment of life? Do you have a sexual peer group? What do you share with them?

8. Some people are appalled by the "promiscuous" and sexually active lifestyle of some gay men. What was your reaction to Ed's description of his life on the circuit of gay bars and discos? Is impersonal sex wrong? How many people do you know who like impersonal sex? Have you ever had impersonal or recreational sex?

9. How would you react to learning that you or someone you loved had AIDS? How do you think your friends and family would react if you were infected with the AIDS virus?

10. Ed initially decided to be sexually inactive but later reactivated his sex life, even though he was infected with the AIDS virus. How do you think you would react, sexually, if you were infected? Do you think it is reasonable to insist that people who have the HIV antibodies stop having sex? What are the ethical and moral parameters that PWAs should follow, in your opinion? Do you think society is doing enough to prevent the spread of AIDS?

11. Ed said he thinks he is ready for death. What did you think of his attitude about death? What does "ready for death" mean to you? If you knew you had a fatal illness, how would that affect you?

12. Even though Ed himself did not want to be tested for AIDS, he now recommends this for people who are sexually active. Do you think people who are sexually active should have the AIDS test? Have you been tested? Are you concerned about your partners and how active they have been? What precautions are you taking, if you are sexually active, to make sure you do not become infected with the HIV virus? Do you know where to go for testing?

13. How did you react to Ed's story about people screaming at him sometimes when he is doing an AIDS presentation and yelling things like "Faggot, why don't you go away and croak"? Do you think society is too intolerant of PWAs? Do you think we should do more to help them?

14. How did you react to Ed's description of public homophobia? Do you know people like this? Do you think it is wrong that people get motivated by a sense of hatred?

15. Ed has developed a very positive outlook on AIDS and how it has affected his life. How would you handle a crisis of this magnitude? Do you believe severe crises can help people sort out what is important in their lives?

16. The spread of HIV has rekindled much debate in the United States about the role of sex education. Currently, education appears to be

the only way to minimize the spread of AIDS. There are many who believe that we are simply not doing enough sex education. What do you think? How would you change sex education in the United States?

17. A highly decorated Vietnam veteran named Matlovich was discharged from the military when the authorities discovered that he was gay. He made legal history by winning court cases to be reinstated. He has since died, and his tombstone reads, "I got medals for killing many men but was damned for loving one." How do you feel about his epitaph?

18. Ed once remarked that the best definition of *promiscuity* was anyone who has had more sexual partners than you have had. Is this definition revealing? How do people use this word?

9
Sex, Drugs, and Rock and Roll: Case Study of Terry Grant

He is more than laid-back. He is relaxed in a way that lets you know he has seen too much. Terry Grant speaks creative hip, not to intimidate, but it's just a lingering reminder of the performance scene that he inhabited. As he is physically unassuming, it is hard to imagine him going all out on stage to wow the teeming crowds, but of course he did. As we begin talking, his bizarre success and socially checkered past quickly come to life.

Terry grew up just outside Houston, Texas, as a single child. His mother and father both worked as public school teachers, and they never showed a great deal of affection for each other. One of Terry's most vivid memories was that of his father's continual and futile attempts to be genuinely affectionate.

> Both my parents were emotionally abused as children. Neither of them were ever really loved by their parents. My mom really learned how to love someone when I was born. She told me that when she first saw me at the hospital she knew she could love me like she had never been loved. My dad always tried to work himself into loving me, but to this day I still do not believe he truly knows how to love anyone. But he did try. He told me he loved me every day, and he always gave me a kiss or whatever when I was growing up. So he did try. It was just somehow he never really made it. He never actually loved me or my mom.

Terry enjoyed being around his mom throughout his childhood. To this day, her gentleness and femininity inspire his idealized images of what women can and, from his perspective, should be. The one distinctive event in Terry's uneventful childhood occurred when he was ten. At that age, he became extremely interested in music, particularly rock and roll.

> When I was young, about nine or ten, I discovered rock 'n' roll, and I really got into it. I would listen to it as much as I could, and I also had a friend with a cheap guitar which I borrowed. I discovered that if I listened to a song once I could pick up the basic sound of it and just work on that until I had what I wanted. I played music constantly, and when I was not playing it myself,

I listened to all kinds of rock 'n' roll as much as I could. Music became my life. I was totally into it—totally.

Terry's increasing interest in music also helped him meet Laureen, his first girlfriend.

It was weird being a kid—like people were always following me around. I could do things the other kids could not. Even at eleven or twelve I could play songs on my guitar, and people would follow me around and listen. So when I was like thirteen or so I met her—Laureen. I met her when I was playing my guitar with a friend, and pretty soon I was just hanging out with her a lot. Then for my fourteenth Christmas present we both jumped in the sack and both lost our virginity at the same time. It was sort of funny really because it only lasted like five minutes. It really did not seem like that big a deal.

In high school Terry coasted through classes, continued seeing Laureen, and most passionately played rock and roll. Terry's passion for rock and roll seemed to give his life direction and purpose. It was exciting, and he immersed himself in the music. He quickly discovered that he was quite good at imitating the top hits as well as creating his own words and music. His exceptional talents proved useful with numerous bands and led to his early career in music.

The first band I was in—these guys were like nineteen and twenty and I was just fourteen. I could play anything they could play. I was like the kid in the group and they all found it pretty funny, my being so young and so into music. Our first gig was at a Catholic church carnival, and it was pretty fun playing for the crowds. We did various shows around our local area, and I stayed with that for about a year. Then I went to a hard-core show in Houston and I met some people and I told them I could play. They said, "Cool," and so we all started playing and I got to know a lot of the people in that music scene. Over the next few years I did gigs with a lot of groups. I even played for a couple of weeks with a group called Tammy Tampon and the Toxic Shock Syndrome. Anyway, it was during this time of playing with so many different groups that I met several of the guys who ultimately formed the group that went to San Francisco and who I finally did my first national tour with.

During this period of switching bands and meeting people in the music scene, Terry also continued seeing Laureen. Emotionally, they were friendly and supportive, but Terry always found it difficult to be affectionate. He cared for Laureen and he enjoyed their sex, but somehow it all seemed mechanical. In spite of these problems, his relationship with Laureen provided some stability in his life. Since he was not interested in school and did not know where his interest in music would lead, Laureen gave him a home base—a sense of security. However, all this changed dramatically on one particular day.

When I was sixteen I got kind of shocked one day when I went over to her house. I had my own key and let myself in one day after knocking and getting no answer; I went to put some of the stuff in her room and oh wow!—she was having sex with her best girlfriend. At that point in time, I finally understood what the much-discussed male ego was all about. I was just totally crushed. I could not even talk to her or anything for over a year.

Days after discovering Laureen in bed with her girlfriend, Terry quit school and against his parents' wishes moved to San Francisco with his band. Since he was only seventeen his parents were quite upset, but he remained determined to do this. Departing, he believed fame and fortune would soon be his. Though ultimately he would have both, he first discovered hard times, hard-core drug abuse, and hard-edged sex.

When I moved to San Francisco, I had these dreams of grandeur. I thought that music was going to take me to the summit right away. What really happened was I lived in a place called The Vats, which used to be the old Hamms brewery, and eight entire bands lived on one floor. We slept on a flea-ridden carpet, and when my money ran out [second week] I went without any food for over a week. I was no good at mooching money. Many people were repulsed by skinheads at that time. So anyway I just went hungry. Finally, Gary [a guy from another band] helped us find the soup kitchens and restaurants that threw out some good food. There I was, eating garbage and sleeping in a flea-infested pit. My dreams looked pretty naive.

We could not get any shows. Everything fell through. None of our contacts panned out. Finally, we started getting some shows. And later we got very popular. Friday and Saturday nights we even started doing three shows. We would open at one club, play the middle band at another and then be the lead band at still another. We started working a lot, and one night I was totally exhausted. So Q from my band said, "Hey, if I can get you up, will you still play?" I said, "Sure." I had seen him shoot speed, so he hit me, and that was my first tweek on speed. And it blew my mind. I thought, Boy, there is nothing like jamming crystal!

Drugs were only one part of Terry's new life-style. Within the world of rock and roll, many factors can coalesce to form a successful group. Terry described the need for a band to develop an interesting persona that fans could identify. Without something distinctive that appealed to young music fans, groups were often ignored. Flash is cash, as the saying goes.

I got quite a reputation for being wild or violent, particularly in the underground newspapers. I would show up in a town and people would ask me, "Did you really do this or that?" and I had never even thought of that before. But of course you would take on some of it because it always got people to the shows. It is all part of the game. *If you want to play the game for big bucks you have to play for the image.* For me, playing at being a wild guy paid off. Lots of groups do something to get the image. Like the Who destroying hotel rooms. Some smashed furniture gets you quite an image. And people go, "Oh wow! That was the Who that did that—we have to go see their show." While this might sound like cheap theatrics, there is a lot of money in this. We were certainly not superstars, but we played with some of the most famous. For a forty-minute warm-up we would make thousands of bucks apiece. The point is, *if you are really suppressed and you have no angle, then the kids are not going to come and see you.* It is just that simple. There are hoards of good musicians out there starving.

Part of the required image for a successful group is their sexual persona. Terry found it hard to build a "cool and wild" sexual image onstage and still be a sensitive, caring lover offstage.

I think like many people, I had an idealized image of womanhood based on my mom—that women are powerful sources of support and nurturing. I also saw femininity as having a creative and gentle essence which was the foundation for building a truly loving relationship. However, in spite of my idealized image of women, I found myself simply using them as sexual objects solely for my own gratification. Within the rock 'n' roll scene we all built up our images or personas, and certainly one did not enhance one's image by linking affection and love with sex. Within this scene, having a regular old lady who you actually cared about was simply being square. If the press found out, you were dead meat.

With the band growing in popularity and playing to larger and larger crowds, the sexual options for Terry's band changed rather dramatically. Many women were willing to have sex with them because of their reputation. For Terry, this became an increasingly vicious cycle of using and being used.

Near the end, when we went into a town we were actually famous. We were not playing twenty-people shows—we were playing to thousands and everybody knew who we were. So sexually it was easy to get whatever I wanted to get. We would go to concerts and scope out who we really wanted for the evening or whatever. Then even before the show started we would talk to them, make them think they were important, then invite them to a party [after the show], and then we pretty much could do whatever we wanted to them. Of course they loved it. It was not just us using them—they liked to brag to their friends that they had made it with X or Y from band Z. Like if we were in town two days, these chicks would go out after balling one of us and call all their friends. So the next night a whole bunch of their friends would show up to see if they could get in on the action. It really happened.

It got to the point where I started hating women because they were using me and I was using them. They were having sex with me just because I was in [the band]. They did not give a rat's ass about me as a person. Sex with these women was like a quick jerk-off—no more, no less. You did it—okay, let us put on our clothes and go back out to party. And the level of insensitivity was phenomenal. People you did not even know were running around calling you their best friend or whatever. There are a lot of lonely and fucked-up people out there who desperately want to be part of this [rock 'n' roll] scene.

As the band became more successful, Terry also started seeing Laureen again. They would try to get together whenever his schedule permitted, but their relationship began to alienate him from the other band members. The need to be more successful and push the music and the group's success still further generated the band's first national tour. This meant leaving Laureen behind and spending even more time with the band.

Being on the road was strange. The last tour I did was six months, with sixty-two cities and Canada too. Even our first tour got to be a drag. I remember the first two months were really cool. I enjoyed being on the road because I was really ready for it. The next couple months were kind of uncomfortable, and the last month or two were highly obnoxious. I hated it. Altogether I spent over three years on the road—the six of us in the band, the roadies, and our managers. It is hard to be with those guys night and day, week after week, and still stay up for the music. The superficial parties and the drugs were also taking their toll.

After the band cut their first album, which was a commercial success, Terry felt the group was pushed to do everything even more intensely. The music had to be more evocative, the group started doing more drugs, and the pressure to be more outrageous increased dramatically. The pressure to be "hard core" reached new extremes.

I did hard-core drugs and I did them in a hard-core way. But in this scene you would do stuff, wild stuff, that you would never do in the outside world. Let me give you an example. This guy in San Francisco owns a theater called Target Video where they make hard-core videos—stuff too extreme for MTV. They shoot the videos, and then they sometimes show them there in their own theater. One gig we were playing in San Francisco, someone from Target wanted to film us—which was okay. So while we were filming, some unknown guy started slashing himself up. So the camera guy just included that in the film. Then they took the camera backstage, and three or four of us were all jilting [inject-ing] speed. So this guy shows up with the video camera and just starts taping us. So my friend squirts a bunch of bloody water at the camera, and the guy films the whole thing. About a week later we were at the theater, and these fools are showing the whole sequence. Well, we were embarrassed, but wherever we went, wherever we were partying, that is the way it was—one wild sequel followed by something more hard core. Whatever you did, the push was always on to be more hard core the next time.

Sexually, Terry's life became complicated. The band's push to be in-creasingly outrageous seemed to increase its fame, which translated into an unending series of "quick, meaningless fucks" for the band members. Terry had his share of meaningless sex, and his escalating reliance on drugs dulled his sporadic relationship with Laureen, and eventually even his music.

I think this is where the sex and drug thing comes together. You see, I came to that point where I did not want women. Like I would get a much better rush out of shooting speed or coke. In all sincerity, I had speed that would give me a hard-on after I jolted [shot] it. So why did I need chicks? I get a better feeling from doing this. And if you did heroin you could not get a hard-on anyway. It just sort of shrank away and you could hardly even see it for a couple of days. It was really a pretty weird situation. I kept doing more and more drugs—always trying to keep the highs high and generally just getting more and more wasted. The work, the road, and the drugs can really do a number on you. And it was totally pathetic to see some of these fabulous-looking chicks shooting up too. With drugs, you have another way of getting whatever you want. Many of these speed sluts had no money, so you would use them, get them high, and send them on their merry way. All this just cheapened the sex act even more. It was a truly weird scene, and I think it just shows how many truly lonely people there are who try to use drugs to relate. It is sad.

After another national tour, the pressure again increased for the group to do more concerts. Although Terry was already making "an obscene amount of money," the record promoters, agents, and most of the band members pushed for an ever-increasing performance schedule. Usually drugged and invariably exhausted, Terry was serving ends other than his own. There is a proverb that warns you to be careful about what you wish for, because you just might get it.

Oh yes, we were big time, but when I was up on stage I felt like a prostitute. You see, I was paid a lot of money to be there and do my gig. And the audience who had paid to have me there could be positive, negative, or indifferent. And because they had bought me for that gig all I could do was put in my time and hope for the best. It usually worked out, but my point is that even when I did not want to work, like if I had been doing speed for days so I only wanted to crash, I still had to go out there and perform for them. I had to put on the act no matter how I really felt, just like a hooker.

While Terry believes rock and rollers face considerable peer pressure to engage in impersonal sex and heavy drug use, he does accept responsibility for staying with the band. Exhausted after this last tour, Terry decided to seek professional help for his drug addiction. With Laureen's help, he took some time out and checked himself into an expensive drug rehabilitation clinic.

Our latest album was doing well, and we were making some serious money. But we were doing more and more drugs. Laureen flew out to Los Angeles to see me, and when she got off the plane she just cried and cried. I was bone white, and she knew what that meant. So my lies were just lies. But she got me to go to the clinic, and it took me about fourteen days to withdraw from the heroin, twenty-one days to withdraw from the coke, and about ten days to withdraw from the speed. I could not do methadone because I was allergic to it, so all they gave me were downers like Valium. Weird, using downers to get over other downers. The clinic scene was painful. Coming off drugs hurts. So I finally got clean, only to go back to speed when I went out on the road again.

During his final national tour, Terry quickly picked up his old routine. He readily admits that no one was forcing him to take drugs, but it was an easy and familiar way to operate in the rock and roll world. Although the drugs kept him going, he became increasingly concerned about how the band members were abusing sex for power. He realized how impersonal and destructive sex can become.

Sex can become such a big power game. It can become an issue of who controls whom. I have known chicks who insist on being on top. They will not do it unless they are the ones doing and controlling it. And of course guys can play power games to get sex and afterwards use it to enhance their own egos. I knew quite a few guys who seemed to enjoy bragging about their latest conquest more than actually being with the woman. Some guys would humiliate their chicks after sex just to push the power game even further. They would pull a "you balled me and now you take all of this grief off me. Wow! I must be damned powerful" trip.

I have seen some pretty shitty things done to women to enhance somebody's power. One night after our show, some Catholic boarding school girl got real drunk and came backstage to party. After Z had her, he told her to put out for everybody backstage. She was real drunk, and they just put a train on her with ten or twelve guys taking turns at her [sexually]. Z thought this was really funny, and he acted like the grand stud of the whole party.

One roadie nicknamed "Backdoor" always used to go at chicks anally. He was pretty rough, and they would always cry out. A lot of the regulars thought that was pretty funny when they would hear one of these women cry out, and they would later tease Backdoor. He ate it up.

After this last tour, Terry decided that he had to leave the band. After resigning, he was quickly replaced. Although shocked and disappointed by how quickly he was excluded and replaced, Terry still does not regret his decision to leave the band and rock and roll. Again with Laureen's help, he began to rebuild his life, to get off drugs, and to learn how to have a loving sexual relationship.

> Laureen began teaching me how to love someone again and how to enjoy sex by personalizing it. All of this felt pretty weird, because basically I had just stopped having sex because it was just totally cheapened. After over three years on the road, sex had evolved into a meaningless gesture. Even the physical release and pleasure were minimal compared to other physical pleasures, and it meant nothing personally. To me, none of the women I was with [on the road] were real people. They were just to be used for getting off. And quite honestly, I never felt that getting off [sexually] with these faceless women compared to a good heroin rush or even the rush of doing a good show.

After several months in another expensive drug clinic, Terry stopped using drugs. He now believes that in some regards the junkie personality suited him. Aware that he could easily return to drug abuse at any time, he remains determined to avoid that.

Terry was never able to reestablish a loving and romantic sexual relationship with Laureen. After he kicked the drug habit, he and Laureen began to fight frequently. In many ways he did not need her or depend on her the way he had before. Since he was no longer a spaced-out junkie, her nursing days were over, and they were not able to build a relationship on an equal footing.

Terry feels that his interests have now broadened. Attending a large state university where he is in the process of finishing his undergraduate degree in philosophy, he finds himself more interested in a wide variety of social issues. Even his interest in music has become more diversified.

> Since I did loud, metal-type music for more than seven years, I am more into laid-back music now. I love reggae music, operas. Oh, I love Wagner. I could listen to Wagner twenty-four hours a day if it was at all possible. I also listen to jazz, blues. I think I really have a much broader scope now.

Currently, Terry describes himself as a practicing existential Zen Buddhist. He believes it is vital to face the immediacy of life's choices, while not wallowing in the past or obsessing over the future. He accepts responsibility for his problems and is now taking steps to improve his life. Next year Terry will begin a two-year stint in Africa, working with the Peace Corps.

I have traveled a long road during the thirty years I have been alive. I have made obscene amounts of money, abused many drugs, and degraded sex until it became meaningless. Sure I have had some good times and good friends, but now I know I have to put my life in order. I want to do something which helps people, including myself. I want to learn to love and respect myself again so that someday I can love again.

ANALYSIS

Sexual Alienation

Terry's story certainly reveals the potential for sexual alienation in contemporary society. For Terry, sex became totally depersonalized and meant so little. All this seems most contemporary and ominous, for traditionally the danger lurking in sexuality has been its potential to mean too much, thereby dominating our lives.

In *Civilization and Its Discontents*, Sigmund Freud talks about how sexual love can be the ultimate source of pleasure. For Freud, the danger of sexual love is not that it becomes meaningless but rather that one can become slavishly devoted to the object of one's affections.

> I am, of course, speaking of the way of life which makes love the center of everything, which looks for all satisfaction in loving and being loved. A psychical attitude of this sort comes naturally enough to all of us; one of the forms in which love manifests itself—sexual love—has given us our most intensive experience of an overwhelming sensation of pleasure and has thus furnished us with a pattern for our search for happiness. What is more natural than that we should persist in looking for happiness along the path on which we first encountered it? The weak side of this technique of living is easy to see; otherwise no human being would have thought of abandoning this path to happiness for any other. It is that we are never so defenseless against suffering as when we love, never so helplessly unhappy as when we have lost our loved object or its love. (1930, 1961, 29)

Clearly this is not a problem in Terry's life, because for him sex was mostly impersonal and did not involve another person whom he really cared about. Terry's case also contradicts the theory that the repression of sexual expression has led to the weakening of eros, or the life-affirming instinct, which may be undermining contemporary civilization itself. Herbert Marcuse, in *Eros and Civilization* (1974), describes how civilization requires the sublimation of sexual expression and virtually insists on the desexualization of modern man. According to Marcuse, this desexualization or repression of basic and healthy sexual urges creates major problems in contemporary society.

> Thus the main sphere of civilization appears as a sphere of sublimation. But sublimation involves desexualization . . . Culture demands continuous sublimation; it thereby weakens Eros, the builder of culture. And desexualization, by weakening Eros, unbinds the destructive impulses. (p. 83)

But again, we see that Terry's problems are not rooted in the denial of sexual expression but instead spring from uninhibited sexual expression with virtually no meaning attached. Much of what Terry has described parallels Karl Marx's early writings on alienation. Marx believed our work environment could alienate us from the natural process of human enjoyment. Marx maintained that work that was inherently alienating, like that found in many capitalist systems, could create an individual level of gratification that becomes solely egotistical and self-centered. For Marx, modern work demands that people give up an authentic way of relating to themselves, to other people, and to the work itself.

In a similar vein Terry described how his work and his need to succeed in a rock and roll band required that he pretend to be many things that ultimately alienated him. In particular, Terry's remark that he felt like a prostitute is indeed reminiscent of some of Marx's early writings on alienation. István Mézáros, in *Marx's Theory of Alienation* (1972), describes how human enjoyment can ultimately become an alienated act and how even basic experiences can cease to have human value.

> "*Human* enjoyment" implies a higher than narrowly individual level of gratification in the spontaneity of experience. Such a level is attainable only because the *humanly* gratified sense is interrelated with all the other human senses and powers in the very act of enjoyment itself. If, therefore, the complex social interrelatedness of the particular senses is disrupted by the "crude solitariness" of egoistic self-gratification, this means inevitably that enjoyment itself loses its general human significance—ceases to be *human*. (p. 203)

The sexual alienation Terry described was caused by a number of factors. By participating in the rock and roll scene, Terry faced strong structural encouragements to discount women and personalized sex. His sex life ceased to have meaning. Carl Jung wrote extensively about various human experiences and how they become meaningful.

> It is only the meaningful that sets us free . . . Experiences cannot be *made*. They happen—yet fortunately their independence of man's activity is not absolute but relative. We can draw closer to them—that much lies within our human reach. There are ways which bring us nearer to living experience, yet we should beware of calling these ways "methods." The very word has a deadening effect. The way to experience, moreover, is anything but a clever trick; it is rather *a venture which requires us to commit ourselves with our whole being to that experience.* (1933, 225–26)

Authentic Experience

For Jung, the critical dimension to authentic experience was the total commitment of oneself to an experience. This is something Terry clearly lacked in his sexual relationships. Terry described many of the women he slept with as "faceless." They had no personality in his world of experience, and consequently he related to them only as vehicles for sexual gratification. This obviously became a vicious cycle of using and feeling used.

Many writers discuss sexuality as a realm of human experience in which we can fully experience both ourselves and our lover. In *Nature, Man, and Woman* (1970), Alan Watts builds a powerful case that the relationship between lovers can be a vehicle for transcending the isolation and feelings of loneliness that self-centered experiences can bring. Watts offers these insights into how sexual relatedness can be a powerful and positive influence in one's life:

> Obviously, the possession of a body is not a relationship to a person; one is related to the person only in being related to the organism of another in its total functioning. For the human being is not a thing but a process, not an object but a life. (1970, 148)

> The sexual relationship is a setting in which the full opening of attention may rather easily be realized because it is so immediately rewarding. It is the most common and dramatic instance of union between oneself and the other. But to serve as means of initiation to the "one body" of the universe, it requires what we have called a contemplative approach. This is not love "without desire" in the sense of love without delight, but love which is not contrived or wilfully provoked as an escape from the habitual empty feeling of an isolated ego . . .
>
> Now sexuality is in this sense abstract whenever it is exploited or forced, when it is a deliberate, self-conscious, and compulsive pursuit of ecstasy. Ecstasy, or transcending oneself, is the natural accompaniment of a full relationship in which we experience the "inner identity" between ourselves and the world. But when that relationship is hidden and the individual feels himself to be a restricted island of consciousness, his emotional experience is largely one of restriction. (1970, 152–54)

I-You World

But the central question remains, How did Terry Grant become so sexually alienated? Martin Buber talks in *I and Thou* (1970) about different ways in which we, as conscious human beings, can relate to the world. Buber, an established Hasidic scholar of the late nineteenth and early twentieth centuries, developed a complex scheme for analyzing how humans relate to the world. Though a number of variations are possible in Buber's scheme, two in particular have an important bearing on Terry's case. The first of these Buber described as an I-It relationship. Buber talks at some length about how we, as conscious human beings, can relate to the world as a series of objects, and when in this I-It mode, we see ourselves as the manipulators and controllers in this world of objects. In the world of I-It, the world of objects exists to be manipulated, and consequently, we come to have little reverence or awe for the manipulated objects. Buber also postulated an I-Thou, or an I-You, world. In this mode, when we open ourselves up to another person, we often become overwhelmed by encountering that person's presence.

> The basic word I-You can be spoken only with one's whole being. The concentration and fusion into a whole being can never be accomplished by me, can never be accomplished without me. I require a You to become; becoming I, I say You. All actual life is encounter. (1970, 62)

Buber believed that to be truly intimate and to have a fulfilling and meaningful relationship, one must be able to relate to another person within this I-You mode. Buber maintained that science and many dimensions of the modern world require us to operate efficiently and effectively in the I-It world. However, fulfillment and meaningfulness are severely limited in this I-It world. Modern humanity, by becoming very efficient and productive within the I-It world, often overlooks or minimizes the I-You world, and therefore alienation occurs. Buber even went so far as to say that primitive mankind, because it had not established a strong or dominant I-It mode, benefited in some ways from the presence of the I-You relationship in everyday life.

> —Then you believe after all in some paradise in the primal age of humanity?
> —Even if it was a hell—and the age to which we can go back in historical thought was certainly full of wrath and dread and torment and cruelty—unreal it was not.
> Primal man's experiences of encounter were scarcely a matter of tame delight; but even violence against a being one really confronts is better than ghostly solicitude for faceless digits! (1970, 75)

Terry's sexual alienation and lack of intimacy are tragic. While no one would describe Terry's life as sexually repressed or inhibited, his ability to have a never-ending stream of different sexual partners certainly did not provide him with any degree of personal satisfaction or intimacy. It is not obvious how we can immediately increase meaning and significance in our relationships, but most people do want a fulfilling relationship. When Father Graddy talked about how sexuality can become cheapened and meaningless, he described the life Terry Grant ultimately came to have.

We have seen throughout these case studies that there is no one specific way in which all people can find sexual fulfillment and happiness, and yet it is also apparent that most people want meaningful sexual lives. The effects of Terry's sexual alienation might be described by something Lao Tsu wrote several thousand years ago: "When men lack a sense of awe, there will be disaster" (1972, chapter 72).

In our last and final case study, we will meet Joanne Sheridan, whose childhood was so traumatized by incestuous assaults from her father that she, like Terry, had problems developing a meaningful sexual life.

References and Suggested Readings

Buber, Martin N. *I and Thou*. Translated by Walter Kaufmann. New York: Scribner's, 1970.

Freud, Sigmund. *Civilization and Its Discontents*. Translated by James Strachey. New York: Norton, 1930, 1961.

Jung, Carl. *Modern Man in Search of a Soul*. New York: Harcourt, Brace and World, 1933.

Lao Tsu. *Tao Te Ching*. Translated by Gia-Fu Feng and Jane English. New York: Vintage Books, 1972.

Marcuse, Herbert. *Eros and Civilization*. Boston: Beacon Press, 1974.

Mészáros István. *Marx's Theory of Alienation*. New York: Harper and Row, 1972.

Watts, Alan. *Nature, Man and Woman*. New York: Vintage Books, 1970.

DISCUSSION AREAS

1. Terry's parents were not particularly loving toward each other or toward him. In what ways do you think your early family life influences your ability later to love another person? How have your parents influenced your ability to love?

2. Terry had a fairly idealized image of women based on his mother, and yet he was unable to reconcile this with his own personal experiences. Who or what helped form your idealized images for men and women? Do you think you have been able to reconcile your idealized versions of men and women with your experienced reality?

3. By the age of nine or ten, Terry was well aware that music would be a major theme in his life. By that age, what did you know about how your life was going to develop? Were there areas or things going on in your own life you knew would ultimately be significant?

4. When Terry was thirteen years old, he met Laureen, his first girlfriend. What was your first girlfriend or boyfriend like? How did this influence your perception of romantic or sexual involvements? Do you think your first girlfriend/boyfriend indicates how your life will develop later?

5. For his fourteenth Christmas, Terry and Laureen decided to have sex together. Even this first experience did not seem significant. How did your first sexual experience influence your overall development? Did the level of intimacy that you had during your first sexual experience parallel your later sexual encounters?

6. Even early in his musical career Terry felt alienated from women. In several of his early groups, an antiwomen, antifeminist stance was taken, particularly by groups such as Tammy Tampon and the Toxic Shock Syndrome. What events in your early life influenced the way you view men and women? Did you have interests in your own life that influence the way you view sex?

7. When Terry found Laureen in bed with her girlfriend, he said he finally learned how easily the male ego can be bruised. How would you have reacted? In what sense does our sexual identity depend on our ability to attract and retain a lover? In what sense is your sexual identity a part of your overall identity?

8. As Terry and his band began to succeed musically in San Francisco, they also became critically aware of the need to develop an angle. Terry described all of this as "playing the game for big bucks." Do you think this playing the game influenced Terry's sexuality? Do you think this was just an excuse for him to have impersonal sex? Do you think it was hard to live in the rock and roll scene and have a caring,

loving relationship? How does your job or planned profession influence your sexuality?

9. Out on the road touring, Terry felt he was performing both onstage and offstage to enhance his band's image. At the same time, he started to hate women and felt that the rock and roll scene was turning him into a prostitute of sorts. Did this argument make sense to you? Did you think this was a realistic complaint? In what sense do you think we are all required to perform? Are you required to perform professionally or sexually?

10. Terry felt the need in his career to become more "hard core." What are the performance standards within your own life? Where do these come from, and do you feel comfortable with them?

11. Terry described how the concerts, being on the road, and drugs all commingled to cheapen sex more and more. What factors in your own life cheapen or enhance your sexuality? What role, if any, do drugs play in your sexuality? Do you believe drug usage ultimately degrades sexual relationships? Is there a difference between using drugs and abusing them?

12. Terry saw sex and sexuality became vicious power games, with people getting seriously hurt. Do you play sexual power games in your own life? How is sex used in your life? In your significant relationships, do you think power and the politics of sexuality have played a major role in determining how your relationships progressed and what they meant?

13. Terry felt he had become alienated from any kind of interpersonal contact during sex. Do you feel you have good personal relationships when you become sexually involved? What can we do to increase the intimacy level of our sexual involvements? How do you feel about impersonal or what some call recreational sex?

14. Terry became dependent on Laureen to help him move beyond the world of alienated sex and drugs, while she became dependent on helping him. In what sense are we dependent on people we love? How have dependencies influenced your relationships? Do you think it is possible to have relationships that do not involve dependencies? How do we know when our dependencies are becoming unhealthy? Do you think most of us have different levels of dependency that appear again and again in our lives?

15. Terry hopes his two-year term with the Peace Corps will give him time to tune in to his own feelings again and to rediscover the importance of personalized contact with other human beings, particularly lovers. What do you do in your own life to help stay in tune

with your own intimate feelings? Do you think there are times in all of our lives when we need time to assess our own personal feelings?

16. In his last statement, Terry mentioned his desire to love again. Do you believe most people want to be in a loving relationship? What do you desire in a relationship? How do our desires actually affect our relationships?

10
Living with Incest:
Case Study of Joanne Sheridan

A s soon as you meet Joanne Sheridan, you know you are going to like her. Her infectious smile, intelligence, and friendly manner give this attractive middle-aged woman a distinctive charm. Her voice is clear and precise, yet gentle. Actually, there is nothing about Joanne that would initially reveal her painful past or her haunting memories.

Joanne was born and raised in the northwest section of Chicago, Illinois. Her mother converted to Catholicism and married her father, who had been raised in a large, extended, Catholic family. Joanne has an older brother named Paul, ten years older than she is, as well as a sister, Wendy, four years older. Joanne's father is a successful traveling salesman, and he virtually ignores his sickly wife, who more often than not is bedridden.

To all appearances, this large extended family seemed to be a happy and cohesive group. Joanne's paternal grandparents lived right next door, and her maternal grandmother lived upstairs. This grandmother, although extremely shy, was the major source of support and comfort for Joanne, including her in many of her domestic projects, such as baking bread. Joanne remembers this grandmother fondly.

Joanne had a disastrous relationship with her parents.

> My mother is extremely weak and ineffectual. She was sick a lot and used her illnesses to retreat from the family and our problems. She is ultradependent on my father and relies on him for everything. My father is externally the highly successful traveling salesman, church leader, and caring family man. Ultimately he is actually a highly manipulative and coercive brute. Glib exterior, cold and hard inside.

Early in her childhood, Joanne was quite fond of her father. She remembers that she and her sister wished their dad could spend more time at home instead of traveling as a salesman. However, these feelings changed dramatically.

> My dad was a real distant kind of guy. As a young girl I remember all of us missed him a lot when he was out on the road. But as his behavior got worse, when he started [sexually] assaulting

my sister when she was six, our feelings for Dad changed. I remember how my feelings changed from missing him and being excited when he got home to fearing him and fearing what would happen when he did come home. Of course, as a kid, I thought something was wrong with me because I kept pulling away. I was not honoring my father the way the church commanded me to do. I really believed this was just my problem, and at that point I accepted by parents' image of me as a naughty troublemaker.

Joanne attended church five days a week, plus Sunday, and was always sent to a private Catholic school for girls. Early in school, the nuns emphasized the issue of sin and corporal punishment. As a child Joanne wondered how original sin happened, and she remembers feeling bad that she was so sinful. These troubling feelings about Catholicism and sin would increase.

While Joanne was still in elementary school, her father began to manipulate situations so that he could violate her personal space. Lengthy hugs, long, forceful kisses, and unwanted fondling started during this period.

My grandparents lived next door, and they went to Florida each winter. Obviously, Dad had access to their house while they were gone. He frequently went next door [to their house] to work on his financial books. And oh, how I looked up to my sister, and I too wanted to go next door with him to "help with the books." So my guilt as a kid came not only from my religious upbringing, but I remember asking him if I could go next door to "help with the books." And for years later I felt I had stood right there in the kitchen and asked for it. But at nine years old, I really had no idea or concept of what would actually occur at that point. My sister and I had never really talked about what happened next door.

So at nine, I finally got to go alone with my father to "help with the books." I remember my grandparents' living room and him lowering those old-fashioned venetian blinds. And I thought, this does not look like "helping with the books," but there I was at nine, physically confronting my six-foot-four, 280-pound father. He sat on their couch and pulled me onto his lap and raped me. He told me to tell him "to stop if it hurts," but he never stopped. And while I was there physically, I think my mind went up onto those venetian blinds and sat there and just felt real bad. You have to understand how much I trusted him. After all, he was my father, for God's sake. After he said, "Tell me if it hurts,"

I fully trusted that he would stop. I just knew he would, but when I told him how much it hurt, he just kept on going.

After this rape, her father frequently forced her to have sex with him. During the next three years, from the time she was nine until almost her twelfth birthday, her father sexually assaulted her. Later, Joanne learned that her father had been sexually assaulting her sister four years prior to his first sexual assault on her and that he continued to assault Wendy until she was almost sixteen years old.

As a nine-year-old child, Joanne still had both a religious and an instinctive sense that his behavior was wrong. However, her father presented it in a glib, jocular manner and laughed off his role in the assaults. He convinced her that talking about it with either her sister or her mother would be a grave mistake for her, since she was the guilty, sinful cause of this problem—a classic blaming of the victim.

Of course, I was always supposed to keep my mouth shut because the information I had would hurt her [Mom]. He told me repeatedly that it would kill her and turn her life into a living hell if she knew what I had done. And of course I believed him, and being very young I also believed I was to blame. As a child, parents are like gods who can do no wrong. And since this was bad, I felt that I must be the source of this sadness.

This internalization of guilt and shame led to Joanne's later self-destructiveness. About a year after her first rape, Joanne tried to talk about it with Wendy, but Wendy refused to discuss it with her. Wendy has continued a pattern of denial and repression throughout her life. Joanne's mother refused to acknowledge what was occurring, and being sick frequently and highly dependent on her husband, she developed several convenient techniques for ignoring it. Joanne's older brother, Paul, who still lived at home, was part of a youth gang in Chicago and spent most of his time "out with the boys." Later, however, Paul discovered in his own therapy that in some ways he had always known about his father's incestuous relationships with his sisters.

For the two and a half years during which she was sexually assaulted, Joanne developed many conflicting and troubling feelings. The conflict over receiving the attention and some physical pleasure mixed with the unwanted sexual contact was increasingly disturbing. Her sense of self-esteem, her emerging sexual feelings, and her own sense of who she was were confused and interwoven within this recurring nightmare of sexual abuse.

Being raised in a strict Catholic school, I received some confusing messages about sex. I really did not know much about the process, even though I had been having sex with my dad for over two years. I thought that when a woman got her period that meant she was pregnant. So at eleven when I had my first period, I just got hysterical. I thought I was having my dad's kid. I remember being in the bathroom screaming up and down that I did not do anything, and Mom is looking at me trying to ignore it all.

With the onset of puberty and after her extreme emotional outburst during her first period, Joanne's incestuous relationship with her father ended. Thinking she was pregnant with her father's child, Joanne panicked. The father, aware that this sort of outburst might ultimately prove incriminating, stopped his assaults on Joanne but continued his pervasive campaign to make her feel guilty, cheap, and sinful. Her mother, whose role in all of this was always uncertain, continued her pattern of strict denial. After her father stopped sexually assaulting her, Joanne gained a great deal of weight. Eating was not only a source of pleasure but, as she describes it, an excellent defense.

I developed a grotesque body. I ate and ate. And most boys would not even bother to look at me. It repelled them immediately. I gained a lot of weight right up through high school, and I used it as a defense. I will tell you, it was a very good defense to keep everyone away.

During the next three or four years, Joanne began trying to sort out what had happened with her father, what it meant to her, and how this fit in with her overall sense of identity. She began to rebel actively against her parents' directives and the church. Her father needed to portray her as a troublesome child, so these youthful acts of rebellion fit in nicely with his scheme to discredit her. He realized that ultimately she might be a potential witness against him. When Joanne was about sixteen, however, several years after her father had also stopped assaulting her older sister, she was approached by her father one last time.

When I was sixteen, he approached me one day on the stairs and wham! Oh, it was like one of those flashes—I remembered it all so clearly. It was just that look in his eye. It was exactly like I remembered it. It brought everything back! My heart started pounding, and I just said, "No! No!" real loud, and I ran down the stairs to my mom. I told her about it, and she does this thing with a sigh and she closes her eyes and she said, "All right, I will take care of it." And I know she told him because he was just

real angry with me for a long time. And then they both told me
never to mention it again.

Later, both of her parents repeatedly encouraged her never to mention
her father's behavior to anyone. Feeling a deep sense of guilt and shame
and knowing that this could indeed ruin the whole family, Joanne kept
quiet. Again, being young, Joanne accepted the guilt and shame for what
had happened.

Interestingly, while her father privately made her feel guilty and
ashamed about the incest, he continued in public to be the outspoken,
chauvinistic male at family and public gatherings. His behavior sent out
very confusing signals as Joanne tried to understand her own sexuality,
her own sexual desires, and how ultimately she would relate to males her
own age.

I never dated or went out in high school. I was real unsure of
myself. The older I got the more afraid I got of boys, and men I
could not take at all. And my dad was always around with his
suggestive remarks and public fondling, but always with this big
smile on his face, doing this stuff blatantly in front of everyone,
and yet his big smile said, "You do not see this—this does not
count." His whole persona is just incredible. He always had a
sexual innuendo ready while making passes at waitresses or
whoever was around. He is the master of camouflage. "You cannot really be insulted by my putting my hand there or saying that
to you." His smug smile tells you it does not count—that it cannot be taken seriously. And with him around the house more and
more, my ability to relate to boys my own age was nil. There was
a vicious self-hatred too—a major part of this incest process. Self-
esteem was a concept totally foreign to my life then. I could not
trust my feelings or instincts—look where they had led me!

Because of her experiences with her father, Joanne came to believe
that of course females should be used by males to gratify their own sexual
needs.

In high school, I thought if someone approached you with a certain smile on their face or that look in their eye, then all they
wanted was a piece of ass. That is what my dad had always
wanted. Why should these boys my own age want anything else?
That is all I had ever really meant to him, and I assumed other
guys were the same.

During high school, Joanne had more and more trouble relating to anybody her own age, particularly boys. She felt increasingly reclusive and less comfortable with herself and her ability to relate to others. She also became hypervigilant about being sexually assaulted and began to spend all her free time in her room at home. After graduating from high school, she secured a job in downtown Chicago at a large bank.

When I got the job at Continental Bank downtown, I just could not keep it. I mean you have to get in an elevator to get up to the fortieth floor and surprise, surprise, both sexes use those elevators. I got to the point where I simply could not get into those crowded elevators with strange men. I really tried—I just could not do it. I had an overwhelming fear that a strange man would attack me right there in one of those crowded elevators. That fear was very real and overpowering for me.

I kept getting more and more reclusive—staying home, hiding from the world in my bedroom. And then I got into this thing where I would paralyze myself—literally make myself immobile. And it got pretty bizarre. And I really went down, down, and down. I could not sleep much or eat. I would get up sometimes just at night to walk the streets of Chicago and go back to my room to hide all day. And finally I had to be institutionalized in a mental hospital. And there was nothing to be done except to have me flip out. Who would believe me, as crazy as I was? My dad, the pillar of the community and good old crazy me. I knew he was not going to get busted for this—one look at me, I was totally incoherent. And my sister would not say anything. I asked her if she would tell them [the authorities at the mental hospital] the truth. She told me she knew I was telling the truth, but she was too afraid of Dad to say anything. I know her fear and cannot blame her.

The next two years of Joanne's life were even more confusing and troubling. In and out of three separate mental institutions or leading the reclusive and highly fragmented life at home, Joanne began to try to figure out how to put her life together. Often heavily sedated in the hospital, she grew to hate her heavy Thorazine schedule.

Joanne became very tired of her difficult life, and in the last state mental hospital she developed a determination not to let her troubled childhood destroy the rest of her life too. She decided to fight back and made a conscious decision to pull her life together. For the first time, she confronted her rage and anger at her father.

I became determined not to let this [incest] ruin my whole life. I figured he simply cannot have that kind of control over me anymore. Fuck him. I am not going to fall apart anymore. I am going to come out of this kicking and screaming. Basically, this was a total and complete rejection of him. I just am not going to be the compliant, nice little Catholic girl anymore. I played by those rules and they did not work. So now I am empowering myself to take control of my life, and my father can just go to hell. And if there is a hell and any justice, surely he will end up there.

After getting released from the state mental hospital, Joanne held a variety of jobs while continuing to live at home. Since she had virtually no self-confidence, living at home seemed like the only available option. Working as a teller in a bank and, later, as an administrative assistant in a law firm, Joanne began saving her money in order to leave her family, Chicago, and her devastating past. By age twenty, with a poor sense of self-worth and self-identity, she also began to try to have some relationships with men.

I thought the only thing I could bring to a relationship was sex. Based on that, I started having sex with a lot of different guys. I would do pretty much whatever they wanted. It was not that I thought I was hot stuff, but it was some attention, better than nothing. I could also talk about it—with them or with my girlfriends. One of the strangest things about sex with my dad was that I could not talk about it—really talk about my feelings with anyone, particularly him. With these guys, I could share my feelings and thoughts about the whole sexual process. And, of course, in some ways it was positive stroking for me (pardon the pun). At least there was some emotional intimacy there with the sex act. Another positive thing about this period of being promiscuous was that I was there by choice. No one forced me to have sex with these guys. I chose to. However, on another level, I was rapidly becoming the slut which I had always been portrayed as. Now my black sheep standing in the family was really being confirmed.

Although she was determined not to return to the mental hospitals and was equally determined to create a positive sexual identity for herself, Joanne began having serious doubts about her ability ever to recover from her abusive home life. Some days life seemed pretty futile. She began thinking about taking her own life.

I was also suicidal during this period. I did some self-mutilations, some cutting on myself. I slashed my wrists up pretty badly once, and another time in the hospital cut my legs pretty viciously. I did not think I really wanted to kill myself, but I wanted to see if I could still feel something physical. I was so disassociated, I lacked so much control, I wanted to know the pain of being connected to my body. I wanted it to be real. I went far enough to really frighten myself.

When she was twenty-three, Joanne met Fred. Joanne's friendship and sexual involvement with Fred proved pivotal in her life. Fred became the person who did help her to escape from her family and Chicago.

I felt Fred was different from any of the men I knew. He had an alcoholic father but was still a kind, caring person. He showed a lot of emotion, and he wanted to spend time with me beyond just the sex. It was something new to me. And he was willing to go away with me because he knew that I needed to get away. That meant a lot to me. I thought it was very romantic. In many ways, I was just young and naive.

At first Joanne's relationship with Fred was fairly idyllic, particularly in contrast to her past sexual experiences. Although at times he was insensitive and uncaring, Fred treated her as more than a sexual object. Since he had grown up in northern Arizona, he invited Joanne to leave Chicago and return with him to the Grand Canyon. Joanne had saved some money, so she left her family, who were mortified that she was running off, unmarried, to live with Fred in Arizona.

Joanne fondly remembers the first year of living with Fred at the Grand Canyon, her relationship with Fred, and how the canyon itself came to have a special meaning.

I just fell in love with the [Grand] Canyon. It is a powerful and spiritual place for me. We got jobs there at the canyon, and we spent all of our free time exploring and hiking it. For the first time in my life, I developed a real sense of myself and of the natural harmonies of the outdoors. I felt alive, young, attractive, and in love, legitimate love. That period was one of great healing and growth. The canyon will always be a profoundly powerful place for me.

After living together a year, they got married to have a baby. When their daughter was born, they needed more money, so they moved to Phoenix. Joanne's savings from Chicago were exhausted, and with a new infant daughter, issues from Joanne's past began to resurface, causing trouble. The effects of her father's incestuous assaults began to haunt her again.

I never denied that it happened. It was just denial of the effect. It just cannot affect me, I kept telling myself. And my life was getting constantly more strained. The longer I was in Arizona the more independent I got, the more I tried to learn about myself, and the more weird it got. My life started to fall apart again.

Joanne developed a series of severe psychosomatic illnesses. One set of illnesses occurred after a particularly lucid dream, which she shared with her new psychiatrist.

I vividly remember being in this circle of light, and the circle was ringed with people. No one I knew—just people—lots of people. I was floating in the middle of this circle of light and people, and all of the people started pointing at me. They started getting angry at me, and they just kept pointing at me and getting madder. They kept shaking their fingers at me, and collectively, without touching me, they forced me to fly out of the circle into a dark abyss which was the only place I could get away from their extreme anger, and all of their pointing fingers. In the abyss, it was totally dark and cold, but I had escaped all of those angry people. When I awoke, my right leg was paralyzed and my knee was so swollen, the doctors were convinced that I had shattered my kneecap. After a million X rays and tests, they finally decided my paralysis and severely swollen knee were mentally induced problems, which I then took up with a psychiatrist.

For the first time in her life, Joanne began intensive counseling to deal with her incestuous experiences. Though she had been hospitalized previously in state mental hospitals, only drug therapy had been used to normalize her behavior. Joanne feels that this intensive therapy was another important step in her overall healing process, and it helped her relate better to herself and to her new infant daughter.

When my daughter was first born, I looked at her, and oh wow! There she was, her own separate being, and ever so vulnerable and innocent. And I looked at her and thought of my parents. How could they treat me that way? I realized that I must have been little and innocent too, with lots of potential, and look what he did with that innocence. And now I have a picture of myself as a baby hanging in my living room, and when I look at that picture, into my eyes, I see something—some good humanness, some good qualities, and I know some of that has survived. I was not the wicked, evil, sinful little girl that I was taught to believe I was.

For the next several years, her therapy helped dramatically. Joanne felt more effective in her various jobs, in her relationship with Fred, and in her new role as a mother. However, after seven years of marriage she felt that the relationship was doomed. Fred was not trustworthy. He had stolen property from several employers, and, more significantly, he did not seem to be open and honest in his dealings with her. Joanne had to have someone she could trust, so she decided to leave him. As an unskilled, single woman, she doubted that she could support her daughter; so she left her young daughter with Fred, temporarily, while she resettled her life.

In spite of her problems at home, Joanne had always done well in school. Deciding to return to school, she secured six weeks of support from the JTPA (Job Training Partnership Authority), during which she planned her return to school with a part-time job at the university. She eventually moved into married-student housing and began, with the help of her therapist, a new and more stable life with her daughter.

During the next several years, Joanne tried various different jobs, and she ultimately became a guidance counselor at a victim services center. Her life with her daughter became increasingly satisfying, and her fears of being an inadequate mother proved to be unfounded. She has had a couple of sexual relationships since separating from her husband, but she is not currently involved. Joanne wants another relationship, but for now there are issues that she wants to sort out with her therapist. She relishes being a counselor and mother.

Shortly after she became a guidance counselor, her maternal grandmother died. Joanne decided to return to Chicago one last time for the funeral.

> The last time I saw him [her father], I went back to Chicago for my grandmother's funeral. I refused to stay at their house because I took my daughter with me. Even though she had been warned by me and my sister, I did not want to take any chances. So after the funeral, we went to the hall [for the wake], and I would not talk to him at all. He got pretty loose [drunk] and came up behind me while I was sitting down and put a choke hold around my neck and tightened it and said, "Tell me when it hurts"—exactly what he said when he first had sex with me—and I replied, "You can never hurt me again, you bastard," and then he just laughed and laughed like it was all one big funny joke.

Several months after visiting Chicago for her grandmother's funeral, Joanne attempted one last reconciliation with her parents. She wanted an acknowledgment of what had happened, and the child within her also hoped for an apology from loving parents which she had always wanted.

Responding, her father sent a certified letter disowning all his children. In his letter he refused to accredit what he termed "any real or imagined events" with which he had been confronted.

> Prior to his severing contact with all of his children, our relationship was dwindling fast and highly strained. There just are not many pluses I can share with you about my parents. I have absolutely no relationship with my parents now. I have had no relationship or any kind of contact with them for over ten years.

Working with her therapist, Joanne now realizes that her father's incestuous assaults have disrupted her entire developmental growth process. On a most profound level, Joanne understands that her fundamental need to be loved and protected as a child was never fulfilled.

> I was in an intense session with my therapist, and she kept asking me what the child within me really wanted and what that child still needs. Suddenly, I burst out crying and sobbed that I wanted my mommy. I wanted and probably still need that kind of unconditional love, for someone to really be there for me and to take care of me and the child within me. Of course, my mom was never there for me and instead spent lots of time pretending not to know about what my dad was doing to me and my sister.

Joanne remains angry about what her father did to her, but she also remains determined to move beyond that anger to have the highest quality life possible. She remains convinced that incest and other forms of sexual abuse are widespread problems that occur more frequently than is commonly acknowledged. For Joanne, the authoritarian tradition found in many religions can foster sexual abuse.

> I think incest can occur easily in a strongly religiously based household. First of all, there is that strong authoritarian attitude that pervades everything, coupled with an edict to honor thy father and mother. Of course, in my Catholic household, children were born with venial sin, born with a black mark against us before we even had done anything. So we were already looked at as somehow sinful. Then there was the classic double standard where boys were just being boys when sexually active, while girls were sluts. And my father had an endless series of slut and whore jokes which he constantly bantered around. Yet, in his world, in his well-defined reality, he has never done anything sexually wrong. I know he believes that. And in some sinister ways, his whole religious environment supports his perception of this.

Based on her experiences, Joanne also believes that most incest victims will not receive much support from their families to confront the perpetrator.

I think incest victims should not hold out much hope that their families will believe them and help them deal with it. At least from my experience, denial was simply too strong. My parents put a lot of energy into denial, and because of that we will never be one family again. I also had to let go of my fantasies about my parents. Just like all little kids, I wanted good and loving parents. But I did not have parents like that, and part of my healing process was letting go of that fantasy—the June Cleavers and all—and facing up to the reality that I really grew up with.

Joanne recently found out that her father's problems had much wider implications than she had initially suspected. Her aunt told her,

Joanne, you are not going to stop it. It has been going on long before you were ever born, and it will continue to go on no matter what you do. He forced me to have sex with him when we were just teenagers, and I just do not believe he can be stopped.

Currently, Joanne had this to say about her life:

Of course I am still angry. But I also came to a realization that I could move beyond my anger, deal with my pain, and regain control of my life. My sister has never come to terms with it, and I do not think she ever will. She keeps trying, but the anger is always there, and she keeps turning it inward onto herself. For me, I could not let him totally break me. Even as a kid, I mouthed off, whereas my sister seemed more docile and less able to overcome her anger and hurt. Her pain and her anguish dominate her life even today, some twenty-five years later. It really is quite sad.

Joanne's current life shows what people can do with childhood tragedies. As a guidance counselor, Joanne has found her work at the shelter a complicated and challenging process. While she is sensitized to the types of suffering and anguish that incest can cause, her very sensitivity can sometimes be too painful.

As a counselor, I want to help my clients, particularly the children. I know recovery is a long process, but I want to be that someone in their lives who believes them and who can tell them it was not their fault. They did not do anything wrong, and they have a right to speak the truth, no matter what the courts say or what their parents say. The seeds of recovery have to be planted.

I am effective at helping in this recovery process as long as I do not allow myself to blur the boundaries between their pain and my own. I also cannot allow myself to become too frustrated due to the structural limitations of society's intervention process. For example, in this state there is no such thing as incest. We legally mitigate the issue by calling it molestation. The truth is, many people simply do not want to face this issue.

While Joanne is still dealing with the long-term process of healing from incest, she is using her traumatic past to build a satisfying life at her job, at school, and with her daughter. She still has some fears and anxieties about men and some anger concerning authority figures. She even has some lingering physical phobias to confront.

Now, wherever I am, I have to identify escape routes. No matter what I do or where I go, I always have to know how I can get away on my own power. For example, I even checked out the exits in this building before I came to this interview. I think this is a big issue with me still—a sort of delayed compensation, because, of course, with my father, there was no escape.

And, of course, I sometimes space out now. I go to a point just outside of my body, just beside myself, where I can be more in control, over there [pointing] where nobody can see me or touch me or hurt me. I just kind of split when I need to.

This lifetime healing process is not easy. Despite anxieties and other tensions, Joanne works diligently and courageously to reach out and help other victims of incest. In closing her interview, she offered the following advice for other incest/sexual abuse victims:

The thing I would say to other incest victims is to acknowledge survival. Ultimately, we are given our own life to live, especially when we become adults; and at that point we can make our own decisions and take charge. As children, some of us were forced into horrible situations, situations which made the world seem like a menacing, oppressive place. And each of us survived as best we could. But ultimately we can, and indeed must, regain and take charge of our own lives.

Many of us play out some very self-destructive roles as former incest victims. But I do not believe that in our hearts we really want to hurt ourselves again and again. Take a good look at yourself and the situation you found yourself in, and sort out how much of your life is just reflexive reaction and how much is really stuff you want to be doing. The question is really about empowerment—how you can take charge of the quality of your life and know deep down inside that you can live with and respect yourself. I have learned slowly and with many stumbles to be comfortable with myself. I am so thankful that I am finally in charge of my life.

Special Note: If while reading this case study you realized that you or someone you care about has been the victim of an incestuous sexual assault, you may want to do the following:

1. Find an experienced and well-respected therapist with whom you feel comfortable discussing your sexually abusive situation.
2. Review the extensive and expanding literature on incest, and select materials that you find insightful and supportive. (See Bass and Davis 1988, 466–86, for a good recent review of this literature and the resources available.)
3. Contact:

   Incest Survivors Anonymous
   P.O. Box 5613
   Long Beach, CA 90805

   or

   Survivors of Incest Anonymous
   P.O. Box 21817
   Baltimore, MD 21222
   (301) 282-3400

   ISA offers peer self-help programs through chapters nationwide. SIA offers specific plans for recovery and has an extensive series of supportive publications available.
4. Find a good friend, physician, teacher, or someone you respect and ask her or him for advice concerning your situation. Remember, you are not the only victim, and there are caring, supportive people who can help you find a recovery strategy that makes sense for you.

ANALYSIS

The Sexual Abuse of Children

The case study of Joanne Sheridan is extremely painful and shocking. It is hard for most of us to imagine how a father could treat his daughter this way. And yet, there is disturbing evidence that incest and child molestation may not be all that rare. In the classic *The Best Kept Secret: Sexual Abuse of Children* (1980), Florence Rush powerfully documents the argument that the sexual abuse of children is not a random, isolated, deviant act. Rather, she asserts, it is a devastating and not uncommon occurrence with many historical and cultural antecedents that foster social toleration, particularly when individual cases occur. Rush argues that although in the abstract the idea of molesting children is abhorrent, there are major themes in both the Bible and Talmud that place overwhelming emphasis on the male sexual drive and on the desirability of young females. She then cites strong empirical evidence showing that some 80–90 percent of molesters are males, 75–80 percent of whom are family friends or family members. So while the idea of childhood molestation is totally unacceptable *in the abstract,* when it does occur and does not involve some unknown degenerate but a close friend or family member, the extreme shame and embarrassment often cause an entire family to deny the incident. This promotes a hellish reality for the child-victim.

Joanne Sheridan's case is typical of cases analyzed by Florence Rush. Her father's jokes about women and his public fondling seem to underscore Rush's point that there are cultural antecedents promoting denial and repression of incestuous assaults. Obviously everyone in Joanne's immediate family knew what was occurring, as did many of her relatives. How could this be tolerated? While it would be easy to dismiss this as an isolated aberration, Rush's argument is much more haunting.

Rape

Another writer who provides added depth for understanding Joanne's case is Susan Brownmiller. In her book *Against Our Will* (1975), Brownmiller demonstrates that rape is usefully understood as part of the basic power inequity between the sexes. Although her forceful argument is too complex to summarize here, her central thesis defines rape as an act of power abuse and as an extension of gender warfare. Joanne mentioned several times how her father not only sexually taunted her and her sister, but even insisted on fondling and verbally attacking waitresses or salesclerks. Indeed his whole public persona was that of the leering male, always trying to show how sleazy and cheap women could be. Ironically, it was his own behavior that proved how insensitive, brutal, and promiscuous people can be.

Symptoms of Abuse

As the title of this chapter suggests, it is a difficult and long process for someone to become a whole person and to develop a positive self-identity after being incestuously victimized. The kinds of guilt, low self-esteem, self-hatred, and physical self-mutilations that Joanne experienced are common. Many victims also have more denial and unrelenting anger than did Joanne. The actual effects of sexual abuse on children are complicated and varied.

David Finkelhor (1979, 1987) contends that child sexual abuse can be usefully incorporated into the current research findings on posttraumatic stress disorder (PTSD). In PTSD a recognizable stressor must be present which would evoke *significant* symptoms of distress in almost any victim. In the PTSD literature the trauma is almost always reexperienced through intrusive recollections, dreams, or sudden overwhelming feelings. The victim almost always experiences a numbing of responsiveness, estrangement from others, hyperalertness, sleep problems, survival guilt, poor memory, or concentration problems. *All* of these symptoms were present in Joanne's case. Finkelhor goes on to identify three basic areas of concern that have to be clinically addressed in cases of PTSD traumatic sexualization: betrayal, stigmatization, and powerlessness. Again, in the case of Joanne Sheridan, all three areas are critical. Finkelhor's modeling of traumatic sexualization predicts that victims of PTSD would need a lot of time to confront and deal effectively with their devastating experiences.

Healing Processes

Ellen Bass and Laura Davis, in *The Courage to Heal* (1988), discuss how important it is for each individual victim of incest to develop a recovery process suitable for herself. Their approach for women survivors of childhood sexual abuse has three phases. First, they suggest *taking stock,* including finding ways to honor what the survivor did to survive. Second, they discuss the ongoing *process of healing,* including learning how to trust oneself, grieving for the betrayal of the child within, and using anger as the base from which to begin healing. Finally, they discuss how sexually abused children can as adults *institute changing patterns* to improve self-esteem, establish intimacy, and build consensual sexual relationships. The book concludes with fifteen studies of courageous women who are learning to live with their history of abuse.

Like the women in Bass and Davis's book, Joanne Sheridan had the courage to face and deal with incest. Sexual abuse/incest does occur in all social strata and under many different circumstances, but haunting patterns of blaming the victim and of overly dependent wives emerge and reemerge. Joanne's case included these recurring patterns too.

Although our discussion and analysis have focused on male abuse of young females, young males are also abused; this appears, however, to be less common. One sensitive, provocative treatment of boys who have been sexually abused is Mike Lew's *Victims No Longer: Men Recovering from Incest and Other Sexual Child Abuse* (1988). I recommend Lew's book to interested students.

The case of Joanne Sheridan is deeply disturbing but such incidents must not be ignored. We must summon the courage to face such traumas and mobilize the support to help these victims find ways to begin healing.

References and Suggested Readings

Bass, Ellen, and Laura Davis. *The Courage to Heal: A Guide for Women Survivors of Child Sexual Abuse.* New York: Harper and Row, 1988.

Brownmiller, Susan. *Against Our Will: Men, Women and Rape.* New York: Simon and Schuster, 1975.

Finkelhor, David. *Sexually Victimized Children.* New York: Free Press, 1979.

———. "Trauma of Child Sexual Abuse." *Journal of Interpersonal Violence* 2:4 (December 1987): 348–66.

Lew, Mike. *Victims No Longer: Men Recovering from Incest and Other Sexual Child Abuse.* New York: Nevraumont Publishers, 1988.

Rush, Florence. *The Best Kept Secret: Sexual Abuse of Children.* New York: McGraw-Hill, 1980.

DISCUSSION AREAS

1. How did you react to the incestuous assault on Joanne? Why do you think this is so alarming and repugnant? Incest is a betrayal on many different levels. What are the different ways in which incest is a betrayal to a young child? How are young children much more vulnerable than adults?

2. Joanne's father did everything in his power to discount his assaults on Joanne and Wendy. Were you amazed at how effectively he manipulated the social reality around his family? Joanne remains convinced that her father's incestuous assaults cannot be stopped. Do you agree? Joanne's father also effectively used an implicit double standard in terms of constructing his version of the family dynamics. He constantly stated that women who are interested in sex are cheap sluts, while males interested in sex are simply being men. Do you think this double standard helps perpetuate these crimes of sexual abuse?

3. Joanne's father quickly made Joanne believe that the sexual assaults were her fault. He appealed to her sense of guilt and shame over the act he perpetrated. Were you shocked to see that blaming the victim actually worked for a while? Do you think this happens in some rape cases as well? Why does society sometimes encourage us to blame victims of sexual crimes (usually women) and not victims of other crimes?

4. Joanne's father convinced her that she should never talk about his assault because it would destroy the entire family. Do you think recent efforts to encourage children to talk about such experiences are useful? Were you, while growing up, encouraged or discouraged from discussing such issues? How would you raise your children on these issues?

5. Joanne used several defense mechanisms to deal with the pain of incest. She talked about spacing out or going to a place outside of her body. She ultimately gained a great deal of weight to prevent her father and other men from being physically interested in her. She even engaged in self-destructive behavior, including self-mutilation and getting involved in some relationships in which she knew she would not be treated well. How did you react to the mechanisms that she used to deal with incest?

6. In high school Joanne reported that she felt many of the boys who looked at her wanted sex. Clearly Joanne's early experiences with her father had colored her perceptions of sex and what people want in a relationship. What do you think most people are looking for in terms

of a sexual relationship? What are you looking for in a sexual relationship?

7. When Joanne began having sex with a lot of men, she said that at least with them she could talk about the sex they were having together. Do you talk about your sexual activities with your lover? If so, does it enhance or detract from your experiences?

8. Joanne developed feelings of ambivalence about her sexuality. While she felt abused by her own father, she did report that the physical act with him after several initial episodes did become pleasurable. This created a great deal of ambivalence in Joanne's life. On the one hand, she knew it was wrong for her father to be doing this, and in some ways she felt she might have encouraged it. On the other hand, there was a certain amount of physical pleasure in the activity. Are you ambivalent about your sexual activity? Do you ever experience guilt over sexual things you have done or have thought about doing?

9. The Grand Canyon and her new relationship with Fred represented a real turning point in Joanne's life. Her romance with Fred as well as the natural world of the canyon combined to create a very positive influence for Joanne. What sort of experiences and relationships have had a strong positive influence in your own life? Do you think physical settings, jobs, and the environment around us influence our personal relationships?

10. Joanne has undergone a lot of therapy to help her deal with her incestuous background. The therapy has helped her move beyond her anger to regain control of her life. In addition to the therapy, what do you think helped Joanne regain this control? Do you think this is possible or impossible for most incest victims? What do you think will become of Joanne's sister, Wendy?

11. Joanne believes incest is often found in authoritarian families and can be promoted by some authoritarian types of religion. Do you agree or disagree? What role did you see Joanne's family playing in her incestuous abuse?

12. As a counselor Joanne believes it is critical to support children when they begin discussing a sexual assault that has been perpetrated on them. She believes such assaults are often compounded by social denial that such events are occurring. Why do you think this occurs? What do you think could be done to correct this?

13. Do you know of anyone who has been sexually abused? How was that situation handled?

14. During her interview Joanne said, "It is amazing how much our sexual experiences color our lives." How have your sexual experiences colored your life?

15. A few therapists now believe the healthiest way to recover from an incestuous assault or rape is simply to minimize the impact such events have on one's life. They say such events should not mean that much. Do you think this would help Joanne deal with her father's sexual assaults?

16. Was Joanne's mother a victim herself, or more of an accomplice in this abuse? Why do many mothers ignore problems like this and discount their children's complaints?

17. One fascinating question about this case is why Joanne has been able to confront her abuse while her sister, Wendy, has repressed it. What variables do you see influencing this dramatic difference in their ways of dealing with incest?

Epilogue

s we have seen in these case studies, the meanings attached to sexual attitudes and behaviors are *highly varied*. The difficulty in interpreting what specific sexual acts or attitudes actually mean has been demonstrated quite dramatically in the recent controversy about President Clinton and Monica Lewinsky. Many Americans as well as numerous commentators from abroad have sought to definitely define what these Oval Office encounters mean. The more speculation, the more options appear. Living in sexually pluralistic times is more than interesting. It offers us the ongoing challenge of creatively reflecting and structuring our own lives so that they become inherently meaningful. In this sense reviewing and thoughtfully reflecting on individual case studies allows us to systematically survey the breadth and depth of contemporary sexuality.

When we consider all ten case studies several important themes emerge. While there are many ways in which human beings experience and develop their sexuality, for most of us, love and romance play central roles in our quest for sexual fulfillment.

We have seen many paths that people use to construct their sexual lives. For many, it is important to pursue sexual passion and the intense intimacy that passion can bring. For other people, seeking a secure and affectionate relationship becomes more important. And many of the subjects in this book sought some balance between passion and security.

When we looked at the lives of the various subjects, we saw how their early family experiences often played a decisive role in their later sexuality. Both Joanne Sheridan and Jennifer Bryce had highly traumatic lives. Incestuous assaults by her father created many problems in Joanne's life. Jennifer's systematic emotional and physical abuse at home clearly influenced her later entrance into the world of prostitution. These kinds of early traumatic problems at home present dramatic contrasts to the kind of supportive family lives that Kevin Krammer and Nick Orren had. Kevin's support from his mother and his father clearly prepared him to develop and overcome his early emotional problems and later to fashion a life he deemed highly successful. Nick's father provided a clear and dynamic role model that Nick found easy to incorporate as part of his own positive self-image, and this ultimately helped him develop what he considered a fulfilling relationship and career.

We also saw how early adolescent themes or problems often have significant impact later in our lives. For Stan Fitzgerald, the decision to avoid the traditional life-style of his parents proved difficult. Patrick Graddy's decision in high school to enter the priesthood ultimately helped fashion his sexuality. For Tori Montgomery, the realization at fourteen of her lesbian feelings helped her begin developing a comfortable and satisfying lesbian life-style.

Although many of our subjects had pivotal sexual turning points in their adolescence, they all continued to grow and change sexually throughout their lives. When her husband committed suicide, Libby Williams was catapulted into a series of sexual changes and emotional developments that she might never have chosen for herself. Nick Orren experimented with a variety of sexual life-styles and partners before ultimately finding a relationship that was satisfying to him. By twenty-five, Jennifer Bryce had decided that the life of prostitution could destroy her. After Kevin Krammer had one marriage that failed and another that deteriorated he had an affair, which helped him become professionally successful and revitalized his second marriage. By thirty, Ed Fogelberg had to try to reconcile his dual themes of religion and homosexuality, as well as deal with his AIDS infection. And last, Terry Grant decided to abandon a financially successful career in rock and roll to begin developing a life that would be more satisfying to him. So again we see that throughout their lives, our subjects have undergone significant changes and reformulations of their own sexuality.

In looking back on the wide variety of experiences our subjects have had and shared, it is obvious that none of them attained their ideal sexual and emotional goals. All the subjects had some painful and traumatic events that influenced their later sexuality. The encouraging side of these problems was that they usually provoked the subjects to find new and more fulfilling ways of being sexual.

As we look back on the particular sexual dimensions of these subjects' lives, we see that so often sex, sexual development, and sexual expressiveness are clearly related to the other dimensions of our lives. In this sense, it seems foolish to study sexual behavior and sexual attitudes while ignoring the other developmental issues we all undergo.

It is also important to understand that human sexuality is not rigidly defined by our biological or physical natures. Sex, as we have seen in the lives of these ten subjects, is a construct fashioned by social mores and norms, by parents and family, by significant others, and by the individual subjects themselves. Sex is an ongoing construction and is often modified and changed within our emergent lives. We all have the ability to reflect and make changes within our intimate lives.

The cases also demonstrate that American society as it enters a new millennium is becoming sexually pluralistic. Indeed, the sexual lives of these subjects are so different from one another that each person really does inhabit a different sexual world. Sexual intercourse certainly means different things to Father Graddy, Libby Williams, and Tori Montgomery. Sexual contact can be as sensually ecstatic as Libby's massage from Dennis, or as traumatic as Joanne Sheridan's experiences with her father. *The variety and power of the meanings we construct in our sexual lives is amazing.*

It is important to recognize this emerging sexual pluralism so that we can move beyond the erotocentrism so common in our culture. Anthropologists are fond of telling us not to be ethnocentric or to make myopic assumptions that our own ways of doing things are the best; likewise, it seems important that we recognize this sexual diversity and acknowledge that each individual must search for his or her own path of optimal sexual development. We should not assume that just because we believe our own sexual life is well configured, other peoples' lives must follow our pattern. We must move beyond erotocentrism. If we do not, we will have to ignore or devalue the wide diversity of sexual life-styles present and confine ourselves to the rigid provincialism and moralism often found in those who do not even try to understand or appreciate other peoples' lives. To accredit only our own experiences is to take a minuscule bite of life.

About the Author

Dick Skeen (Ph.D.) is a professor of sociology at Northern Arizona University. He lives with his wife Janet in the Coconino forest of Flagstaff, Arizona.

Lightning Source UK Ltd.
Milton Keynes UK
UKHW011226260121
377699UK00001B/271